国际邮轮乘务管理专业系列教材

中国高等院校邮轮人才培养联盟　　组织
国际邮轮乘务专业教学协作中心　　编写

邮轮宾客服务双语实训指导

主　编 / 姚丹丽
副主编 / 岑人宁　马　盟
主　审 / 程爵浩

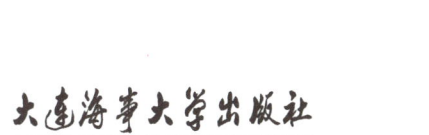

ⓒ 姚丹丽　2025

图书在版编目(CIP)数据

邮轮宾客服务双语实训指导：汉文、英文 / 姚丹丽主编. — 大连：大连海事大学出版社, 2025.8. (国际邮轮乘务管理专业系列教材). — ISBN 978-7-5632-4745-5

Ⅰ. U695.1

中国国家版本馆 CIP 数据核字第 2025T8D718 号

大连海事大学出版社出版

地址：大连市黄浦路523号　邮编：116026　电话：0411-84729665(营销部) 84729480(总编室)
http://press.dlmu.edu.cn　E-mail:dmupress@dlmu.edu.cn

大连金华光彩色印刷有限公司印装	大连海事大学出版社发行
2025年8月第1版	2025年8月第1次印刷
幅面尺寸:184 mm×260 mm	印张:15
字数:330千	印数:1~3000册

出版人：余锡荣

责任编辑：张　冰	责任校对：史云霞
封面设计：解瑶瑶	版式设计：解瑶瑶

ISBN 978-7-5632-4745-5　　定价:49.00元

序

当今,邮轮旅游作为一种时尚和热门产业,正在向着现代社会的每个角落渗透,改变着人们传统的旅游观念。随着中国经济的高速发展,中国的邮轮旅游业顺天时、应地利、聚人和,进入持续发展的快车道。乘坐邮轮出境游这一新兴旅游方式,在中国受到越来越多人的青睐,从2005年仅有几千人,到2014年已经突破70万人,2015年预计突破100万人。未来中国将成为全球最大的邮轮市场之一,增长空间巨大。

受国家旅游局委托,中国交通运输协会邮轮游艇分会(CCYIA)编制的《中国邮轮旅游发展总体规划》(简称《规划》)出台,《规划》提出的发展要点之一是邮轮人才培养教育体系的建立与完善。2014年8月23日,"美国皇家加勒比邮轮公司人才培训中心"在位于天津海河教育园区内的天津海运职业学院正式揭牌。在这一背景下,为规范邮轮专业人才的教育培养,在中国交通运输协会邮轮游艇分会指导下,全国交通运输职业教育教学指导委员会航海类专业指导委员会与中国高等院校邮轮人才培养联盟和国际邮轮乘务专业教学协作中心共同组织相关院校专门为国际邮轮与旅游管理专业学生编写了"国际邮轮乘务管理专业"系列教材。

系列教材共计24种,具体为《邮轮餐饮服务管理》《邮轮休闲娱乐服务管理》《邮轮英语视听说教程》《邮轮客舱服务管理》《邮轮服务礼仪》《邮轮服务英语》《邮轮烹饪英语》《邮轮面试英语》《邮轮基础英语》《邮轮乘务员职业道德与素养》《邮轮服务心理学》《邮轮概论》《邮轮旅游市场营销》《邮轮酒吧服务管理》《邮轮旅游地理》《邮轮卫生与健康》《邮轮旅游业法律基础及案例分析》《邮轮英语词汇手册》《邮轮休闲娱乐服务双语实训指导》《邮轮客舱服务双语实训指导》《邮轮宾客服务双语实训指导》《鸡尾酒调制双语实训指导》《邮轮餐饮服务双语实训指导》《邮轮购物服务双语实训指导》。

系列教材的编写汲取了学术界相关知识、理论和研究成果,参考了大量相关文献资料,深度融合了专业资源库而进一步立体化,力求体例清晰、内容新颖、图文并茂、重点突出,并注重系列教材之间的互相配合,适用于高等院校邮轮人才培养,也可作为邮轮旅游从业人员的参考用书。

系列教材的编写和出版得到了大连海事大学出版社和天津海运职业学院的鼎力支持,中国交通运输协会邮轮游艇分会副会长程爵浩教授对系列教材的编写框架、体例、取舍等提出了很多指导性建议及中肯的、建设性的修改意见,在此表示感谢。

由于水平有限,加之时间特别仓促,不妥之处在所难免,敬请有关专家、读者指正!

郑炜航
2015年8月

前言

随着全球旅游业的迅猛发展，邮轮旅游作为一种高端且惬意的旅行模式，正日益受到广大宾客的追捧。随着中国经济的高速腾飞以及民众生活水平的显著提升，越来越多的中国消费者开始留意并选择邮轮旅游。中国首艘国产大型邮轮"爱达·魔都号"于2024年1月1日正式开启商业首航，截至目前已顺利完成多个航次，为大量宾客提供了优质服务。这一标志性事件意味着中国在国产大型邮轮领域取得重大突破，不仅有力推动了旅游业及相关服务业的进步，还充分彰显了中国制造的实力与创新精神。

邮轮宾客服务管理作为邮轮旅游的关键环节，对于提高宾客满意度、增强邮轮公司竞争力起着至关重要的作用。《邮轮宾客服务双语实训指导》致力于通过系统的理论教学与实践操作，以双语教学的形式，助力学生掌握邮轮宾客服务的核心技能与知识，提升其双语沟通能力和跨文化交际能力，从而满足邮轮旅游业对高素质、国际化专业人才的需求。本书紧密结合现代邮轮宾客服务管理活动的实际开展情况，从邮轮前厅部概要、登离船服务、礼宾服务、前台接待服务、岸上观光服务、未来航程服务、邮轮收银服务、邮轮升舱换舱等八大模块展开详细介绍。进一步细化为十九个项目、三十四个任务。

本教材由浙江交通职业技术学院的姚丹丽副教授担任主编，广西国际商务职业技术学院的岑人宁和浙江交通职业技术学院的马盟老师担任副主编，中国交通运输协会邮轮游艇分会副会长程爵浩教授担任主审。模块一由浙江交通职业技术学院的潘璐瑶老师编写并制作教学资源；模块二和模块六由山东海事职业学院的韩秀秀和牟佳佳老师编写并制作教学资源；模块三由浙江交通职业技术学院的杨晶晶、姚丹丽老师以及武汉交通职业学院的廖莎老师共同编写并制作教学资源；模块四由广西国际商务职业技术学院的岑人宁、朱子豪、罗琰蔚、刘宝玲、庞中燕、宁芮、谢宝茵、林思伶、黄海琼、李莲花等老师共同编写并制作教学资源；模块五由浙江交通职业技术学院的姚丹丽和马盟老师共同编写并制作教学资源；模块七和模块八由福建船政交通职业学院的张力老师编写并制作教学资源。全书由姚丹丽、许梦瑶两位老师修订统稿。中国江苏国际经济技术合作集团有限公司人力资源分公司船员管理中心主任屠小刚先生，船员管理中心经理阮亚威先生为本书内容框架的构建提供了指导与帮助。各参编院校的师生为本书的编写贡献了丰富的案例和资料，同时本书还引用了一些相关资料，在此向相关单位和个人一并致以诚挚的感谢。

教材采用英汉双语模式，尤其注重融入邮轮上的中国文化与元素，以更好地契合行业发展趋势。期望本书能够成为邮轮公司及相关从业人员学习和掌握邮轮宾客服务管理知识的得力助手。由于编者水平有限且时间仓促，本书难免存在不足之处，恳请读者朋友和各位专家批评指正。未来，我们将持续关注邮轮旅游业的发展动态与市场需求，不断优化和完善教材内容，为培养更多优秀的邮轮服务人才而全力以赴。

编者
2025年2月

目 录

模块 1　邮轮前厅部概要 ··· 3

Module 1　Introduction：the Cruise Guest Services Department ······ 3

项目 1　邮轮前厅部概要 ·· 5

Project 1　Introduction：the Cruise Guest Services Department ········· 5

任务 1　邮轮前厅部的主要任务 ··· 5

Mission 1　The Main Tasks of the Cruise Guest Services Department ······ 5

任务 2　邮轮前厅部的组织机构 ·· 13

Mission 2　The Organizational Structure of the Cruise Guest Services Department ······ 13

任务 3　邮轮前厅部员工的素质要求 ·· 24

Mission 3　The Quality Requirements for the Cruise Guest Service Staff ······ 24

模块 2　登离船服务 ·· 43

Module 2　Boarding and Disembarkation Service ···················· 43

项目 1　登船准备工作 ·· 45

Project 1　Preparation for Boarding ··· 45

任务 1　登船手续所需信息 ·· 45

Mission 1　Information Required for Boarding Procedures ············· 45

项目 2　登船服务流程 ·· 50

Project 2　Boarding Service Process ··· 50

任务 1　散客登船 ·· 50

Mission 1　Individual Guests Board the Ship ······························ 50

任务 2　团队宾客登船 ·· 56

Mission 2　Group Guests Board the Ship ·································· 56

项目 3　登船服务实例 ·· 63

Project 3　Examples of Boarding Service ··································· 63

任务 1　在线登记 ·· 63

Mission 1　Online Registration ··· 63

项目 4　登船常见问题处理 ·· 70

Project 4　Handling of Frequently Asked Questions about Boarding ······ 70

任务 1　常见问题处理	70
Mission 1　Handling of Frequently Asked Questions	70
项目 5　邮轮离船服务	75
Project 5　Cruise Disembarkation Service	75
任务 1　邮轮离船服务	75
Mission 1　Cruise Drsembarkation Service	75

模块 3　礼宾服务　79
Module 3　Concierge Service　79

项目 1　行李服务	81
Project 1　Luggage Service	81
任务 1　登船行李托运	81
Mission 1　Luggage Check-in for Boarding	81
任务 2　离船行李托运	85
Mission 2　Disembarkation Luggage Consignment	85
项目 2　贵宾服务	89
Project 2　VIP Service	89
任务 1　了解邮轮贵宾服务	89
Mission 1　Knowing Cruise VIP Services	89
项目 3　礼宾服务常见问题处理	95
Project 3　Common Problems Handling in Concierge Services	95
任务 1　常见案例分享	95
Mission 1　Common Case Sharing	95

模块 4　前台接待服务　103
Module 4　Reception Service　103

项目 1　前台接待	105
Project 1　Reception	105
任务 1　认识邮轮前台	105
Mission 1　The Introduction of Cruise Reception Desk	105
任务 2　换舱服务	109
Mission 2　Cabin Reassignment Service	109
任务 3　问讯服务	114
Mission 3　Inquiry Service	114
任务 4　总机服务	117
Mission 4　Operator Service	117
任务 5　收银服务	121
Mission 5　Cashier Service	121

任务 6　客诉处理 ·· 125
　　Mission 6　Guest Complaint ·· 125
　项目 2　前台接待服务常见问题处理 ··· 129
　Project 2　Handling the Common Problem of Reception Service ············ 129
　　任务 1　常见案例分享 ··· 129
　　Mission 1　Common Case Sharing ·· 129

模块 5　岸上观光服务 ··· 139
Module 5　Shore Excursion Service ·· 139
　项目 1　认识岸上观光服务 ··· 141
　Project 1　Know about Shore Excursion Service ································ 141
　　任务 1　岸上观光部门职责 ·· 141
　　Mission 1　Duty of Shore Excursion Department ····························· 141
　　任务 2　组织岸上观光行程 ·· 146
　　Mission 2　Organize Shore Excursion Itineraries ····························· 146
　项目 2　岸上观光服务常见问题处理 ··· 150
　Project 2　Handling Common Issues in Shore Excursion Services ·········· 150
　　任务 1　常见案例分享 ··· 150
　　Mission 1　Common Case Sharing ·· 150

模块 6　未来航程服务 ··· 157
Module 6　Future Cruise Service ·· 157
　项目 1　未来航程线路 ··· 159
　Project 1　Future Cruise Itinerary ·· 159
　　任务 1　未来航程线路设计 ·· 159
　　Mission 1　Future Cruise Itinerary Design ····································· 159
　项目 2　未来航程销售 ··· 164
　Project 2　Future Cruise Sales ··· 164
　　任务 1　未来航程推介 ··· 164
　　Mission 1　Future Cruise Promotion ··· 164
　　任务 2　未来航程舱房推介 ·· 168
　　Mission 2　Future Cruise Cabin Promotion ···································· 168
　项目 3　未来航船预订 ··· 173
　Project 3　Future Ship Reservation ··· 173
　　任务 1　未来航程船票预订 ·· 173
　　Mission 1　Reservations for Future Cruise Tickets ·························· 173

模块 7　邮轮收银服务 ·· 181
Module 7　Cruise Bill Settlement ·· 181

项目 1　邮轮收银基础 ·· 183
Project 1　Foundation of Cruise Bill Settlement ································ 183

任务 1　外币真假鉴别 ··· 183
Mission 1　Identification of Foreign Currency Authenticity ············· 183

任务 2　外币兑换 ·· 188
Mission 2　Foreign Currency Exchange ····································· 188

任务 3　登记信用卡 ··· 191
Mission 3　Credit Card Registration ··· 191

任务 4　船上付款方式 ··· 195
Mission 4　Payment Method on Cruise ····································· 195

项目 2　邮轮结账 ··· 199
Project 2　Cruise Check-out ··· 199

任务 1　邮轮结账 ·· 199
Mission 1　Cruise Check-out ·· 199

模块 8　邮轮升舱换舱 ·· 205
Module 8　Cruise Ship Upgrade and Cabin Exchange ·························· 205

项目 1　邮轮升舱换舱服务 ··· 207
Project 1　Cruise Ship Upgrade and Cabin Exchange Service ················ 207

任务 1　邮轮升舱服务 ··· 207
Mission 1　Cruise Cabin Upgrade Service ·································· 207

任务 2　邮轮换舱服务 ··· 213
Mission 2　Cruise Cabin Exchange Service ································· 213

附录　邮轮前厅英语词汇 ·· 219
Appendix　English Vocabulary of Cruise Front Office ·························· 219

参考文献 ·· 227
References ·· 227

模块 1

邮轮前厅部概要

Module 1

Introduction: the Cruise Guest Services Department

项目 1 邮轮前厅部概要
Project 1 Introduction: the Cruise Guest Services Department

任务 1 邮轮前厅部的主要任务
Mission 1 The Main Tasks of the Cruise Guest Services Department

实训目的 Training Objectives

教师对邮轮前厅部进行讲解,并引导学生阅读分析相关资料,让学生深入理解邮轮前厅部的运作、重要性以及员工在其中所扮演的角色,进而使学生能够:

The teacher explains the cruise guest services department and guides students to read and analyze relevant materials. This helps students gain a deep understanding of the operation and significance of the cruise guest services department, as well as the roles that employees play in it. As a result, students are able to:

1.阐述邮轮前厅部的概念。

State the concept of the cruise guest services department.

2.举例说明邮轮前厅部的主要工作任务。

Illustrate the main tasks of the cruise guest services department.

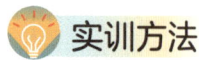

实训方法
Training Method

首先由教师进行讲解，然后学生阅读分析资料。在小组讨论中，教师引导学生进行思考、分析和总结，达到熟练掌握该学习内容的目的。

The process begins with the teacher's explanation, followed by students analyzing reading materials. During group discussions, the teacher guides students to think, analyze, and summarize, aiming to enable them to master the learning content proficiently.

实训准备
Training Preparation

阅读资料1：漂浮在海上的"酒店"还是"度假村"？
Material 1：A "Hotel" or "Resort" Floating on the Sea？
阅读资料2：从乘务长到宾客服务，变的不只是名称。
Material 2：From Pursers to Guest Services, it's more than just a change of name.

实训内容及操作标准
Training Content and Operating Standards

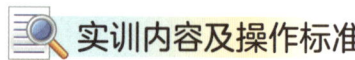 邮轮前厅部的概念

The Concept of the Cruise Guest Services Department

阅读资料1（Material 1）：

漂浮在海上的"酒店"还是"度假村"？
A "Hotel" or "Resort" Floating on the Sea？

如今，邮轮为人们带来了一种全新的旅行方式。吃、住、行、游、娱、购等活动都在船上进行，还能将宾客送至其他目的地供其上岸游玩。宾客无须经历舟车劳顿与长途跋涉，一路上，有的是精致美味的食物、精彩纷呈的运动项目、惬意悠然的咖啡时光、令人乐翻天的娱乐节目，以及有趣实用的学习课程。整个旅途轻松又舒适，让人不自觉便沉醉其中，达到"不知今夕何夕"的状态。正因如此，邮轮被称作漂浮在海上的"度假村"。

Today's cruise ships offer a brand-new way of traveling experience, where dining, accommodation, transportation, sightseeing, entertainment, and shopping all take place on the ship. They also transport guests to other destinations for shore excursions. There is no weariness from arduous journeys or long treks; instead, there are exquisite and delicious foods, exciting sports activities, pleasant coffee breaks, hilarious and exciting shows, and interesting and practical learning courses. The entire journey is easygoing and comfortable, allowing one to unconsciously reach a state of carefree enjoyment, not knowing what day it is. Thus, cruise ships are referred to as "resorts" floating on the sea.

在被称作漂浮在海上的"度假村"之前,邮轮曾一度被称为漂浮在海上的"酒店"。究其原因,一方面,当邮轮作为新鲜事物刚进入中国时,人们对它的认识与了解尚不够深入,便自然而然地将其与酒店联系起来;另一方面,邮轮公司对邮轮部门的划分也容易使人产生误解。邮轮通常由三大部门构成:航海部、市场部和酒店部。邮轮的酒店部所提供的服务,基本上和酒店一致,涵盖客房、前台接待、餐饮、娱乐等方面,因此邮轮被理所当然地称作漂浮在海上的"酒店",这也正是邮轮"前厅部"叫法的由来。此外,为便于人们理解,邮轮中介公司在员工招聘时直接采用"前厅部"这一称呼,在一定程度上进一步扩大了该称谓的影响力。

Before being called "resorts" floating on the sea, cruise ships were once referred to as "hotels" floating on the sea. This was partly due to the fact that when cruise ships first entered China as a new concept, people did not have a deep understanding of them and instinctively associated them with hotels. However, it was also partly because of the misconception caused by the division of departments within the cruise companies. Generally, a cruise ship consists of three main departments: the navigation department, the marketing department, and the hotel department. The services provided by the hotel department of a cruise ship are basically the same as those of a hotel, including guest rooms, front desk reception, catering, entertainment, etc. Therefore, it was naturally referred to as a "hotel" floating on the sea, which is also the origin of the term "front office" in cruising. Additionally, in order to make it easier for people to understand, cruise intermediary companies directly used the term "front office" during recruitment, which also expanded the influence of this term to a certain extent.

邮轮前厅部与酒店前厅部极为相似,它设立于邮轮大堂,承担着招呼、接待宾客的职责,提供登船与离船协助、收银、外币兑换、咨询解答、委托代办以及处理投诉等服务,同时致力于与宾客构建良好关系。

The cruise guest services department is very similar to that of a hotel. Located in the cruise ship's lobby, it is responsible for greeting and receiving guests, providing services like boarding and disembarkation assistance, cashier service, foreign currency exchange, consultation, errand service, and handling complaints, while also building good relationships with guests.

与酒店前厅部相比,邮轮前厅部的功能和职责存在差异。例如,邮轮前厅部并不承担客房预订工作,也没有迎宾服务,其入住接待服务由岸上接待人员和船上接待人员共同完成。

Compared with the front office of a hotel, the functions and responsibilities of the cruise guest services department differ. For example, the cruise guest services department is not responsible for room reservations, nor does it provide a greeting service. The check-in reception service is jointly completed by shore receptionists and ship receptionists.

在行业与学术界，对于邮轮"前厅部"的称谓并不统一。荷美邮轮直接沿用酒店"前厅部"的叫法，其英文名称为"front office department"；公主邮轮则遵循早期船只的传统称呼，英文名称是"pursers department"，该名称既可以译为"事务部"，也可以译为"前厅部"；而大多数邮轮，诸如嘉年华邮轮、皇家加勒比邮轮、精致邮轮、迪士尼邮轮、诺唯真邮轮、地中海邮轮、银海邮轮、世鹏邮轮，均采用"cruise guest services department"来替代"前厅部"的称呼，意为"宾客服务部"。为便于读者理解，本书主要采用邮轮前厅部（cruise guest services department）这一叫法。

Within the industry and academic circles, there is no uniform term for the "front office" of a cruise ship. Holland America directly adopts the English name front office department. Meanwhile, Princess Cruises follows the traditional terminology of early ships, with the English name being pursers department, which can be translated as affairs department or front office department. Most cruise lines, such as Carnival Cruises, Royal Caribbean Cruises, Celebrity Cruises, Disney Cruises, Norwegian Cruises, MSC Cruises, Silversea Cruises, and Seabourn Cruises, use cruise guest services department, which means the guest services department is used instead of the traditional term front office department. For the convenience of readers' understanding, this book mainly uses the term "cruise guest services department" to refer to the front office department of a cruise ship.

三、邮轮前厅部的主要工作任务
The Main Work Tasks of the Cruise Guest Services Department

阅读资料2（Material 2）：

从乘务长到宾客服务，变的不只是名称
From Pursers to Guest Services, It's More Than Just a Change of Name

早在14世纪初，"Purser"（乘务长）这一职务就被列入皇家海军准尉军衔序列，并且作为海军军衔一直沿用到1852年。乘务长主要负责船上物资的管理工作，所涉物资包括食物、酒水、衣物、被褥，甚至蜡烛。乘务长最初被称作"会计员"。在采购过程中，他们通常会从供货商处收取5%的佣金并做好记录，而当把货物转售给船员时，则会适当加价。实际上，乘务长并不负责给船员发放薪水，但却需要密切留意这方面情况，因为船员得支付自身生活开销，而从船员的工资中扣除相应消费款项正是乘务长的职责之一。尽管担任乘务长这一职务没有固定薪酬，但由于有着颇为可观的预期收入，在当时该职位相当抢手。随着船只旅行衍生出越来越多的副业，乘务长也愈发富有。

The title of Purser was included in the Royal Navy's warrant officer rank as early as the 14th century and continued as a naval rank until 1852. The Purser was primarily responsible for the management of supplies on board, such as food, drink, clothing, bedding, and even candles. Initially known as the "accountant", they would typically collect a 5% commission from suppliers during purchases and record it. Goods were sold to the crew members with an appropriate markup. Although the Purser did not handle the crew's salaries, they had to pay close attention because the crew had to cover their living expenses, and deducting their spending from their wages was part of the Purser's job. Although the position of Purser was unpaid, it was highly sought after due to its considerable expected income. As ship travel led to an increasing number of side businesses, Pursers became wealthier.

在现代客运船只上,事务部已发展成为一个由多名员工组成的部门,主要负责处理船上的行政事务、财务税费、外币兑换,以及其他所有与宾客和船员财务相关的事项。随后,随着邮轮业的迅猛发展与广泛普及,乘务长的工作职责进一步转变,主要为邮轮宾客提供登船与离船协助、接待、咨询解答、收银结账、投诉处理等各类服务。20世纪90年代末,许多邮轮开始用"guest services"取代"pursers"这一称谓。这一名称的变更,更多地反映出该部门工作内容和职责的演变,同时也更为直观、准确且形象地展现了该部门的服务对象与工作职责。

In modern guest ships, the Pursers Department has evolved into a department staffed by multiple members, mainly handling on board administrative affairs, financial taxes, foreign currency exchange, and all other matters related to the finances of guests and crew members. Later, with the rapid development and popularization of the cruise industry, the job responsibilities of pursers further evolved, mainly providing services for cruise guests such as boarding assistance and disembarkation assistance, reception, answering inquiries, check-out and cashier service, and complaint handling. In the late 1990s, many cruise lines began to replace pursers with guest services, a name change that more accurately reflects the department's work content and responsibilities, and more vividly and precisely expresses the department's service recipients and job responsibilities.

前厅部处于邮轮接待服务的最前沿,其工作涉及面广泛,业务繁杂,在整个邮轮酒店部的运营过程中,发挥着不可替代的关键作用,承担着极为重要的接待职责。前厅部的主要工作任务涵盖:未来航程销售、提供各类面向宾客的服务、开展协调与沟通工作、进行信息收集与处理、管理客账、建立宾客历史档案,以及负责邮轮会员俱乐部的运营管理等。

The guest services department is at the forefront of cruise ship reception services, with a wide range of services and complex operations. It plays an irreplaceable role in the entire operation process of the cruise hotel department, bearing significant reception tasks. The main work tasks of the guest services department include sales of future cruises, providing various guest services, coordination and communication, information collection and processing, guest account management, establishment of guest history files, management of the cruise membership club, etc.

(一) 未来航程销售
Sales of Future Cruises

未来航程销售是邮轮运营的首要任务之一。邮轮的收入主要来源于船票收益以及船上宾客的消费收入这两大板块。由于客房这类商品具有不可储存性,属于一种"极易损耗"的商品,故而邮轮公司通常会提前半年甚至一年公布次年的航班信息。此举旨在鼓励邮轮宾客提前规划出行计划,如此一来,既能保障船票收益,又能确保船上宾客的消费收入。因此,邮轮前厅部员工务必具备强烈的营销意识与出色的推销能力,积极开展未来航程销售工作。

The sales of future cruises is one of the primary tasks of a cruise ship. The main sources of revenue for a cruise include ticket income and on board guest spending (ON BOARD REVENUE). Due to the non-storable characteristic of cabin products, they are considered a type of "perishable product." Therefore, cruise companies usually announce the sailing information for the following year six months or even a year in advance. The purpose is to encourage cruise guests to plan their trips early, which not only ensures ticket revenue but also guarantees on board guest spending. As a result, the cruise guest service staff must have a strong marketing awareness and sales ability, actively engaging in the sales of future cruises.

(二) 提供各类面向宾客的服务
Providing Various Guest Services

前厅部是邮轮上的一线部门,直接向宾客提供各类相关服务。服务范畴涵盖收银结账、委托代办服务、行李搬运服务、贵宾接待、未来航程销售、投诉处理等,同时还包括协助换房、提供咨询服务、保障电话通信服务、组织岸上观光活动、配备导游服务、开展物品租赁业务以及进行外币兑换等方面。

The front office department is a front-line department on the cruise ship, directly providing various services to guests. The scope of services includes cashiering, errand services, luggage services, VIP reception, future cruise sales, complaint handling, assistance with room changes, consultation services, telephone services, shore excursions, providing tour guide services, item rental, foreign currency exchange.

在提供前厅各项服务的过程中,前厅服务应与邮轮酒店部的其他服务,诸如客舱服务、餐饮服务、安全服务等协同配合,共同构成邮轮酒店部的整体服务体系。要注重服务的全面性与到位程度,让宾客对邮轮之旅留下满意且深刻的印象。

In the process of completing various services of the front office, its services should work together with other services of the cruise hotel department, such as cabin services, catering services, safety services, etc. Efforts should be made to ensure the comprehensiveness and effectiveness of services, leaving guests with a satisfying and profound impression of the cruise.

(三) 开展协调与沟通工作
Coordination and Communication

前厅部依据宾客需求以及邮轮营销部门的销售计划,承担起衔接前、后台业务的职责,同时负责与宾客、旅行社、港口、海关之间的联络与沟通工作,以达成让宾客满意、保障内部业务顺畅运作的目标。举例来说,若宾客向前厅部员工反馈客舱温度存在问题,前厅服务人员需即刻通过管理渠道将宾客意见传达给设备维护部门,并给予宾客一个圆满的答复。

The guest services department connects front-end and back-end businesses and is responsible for the liaison and communication with guests, travel agencies, ports, and customs according to the needs of guests as well as the sales plans of the cruise marketing department, ensuring guest satisfaction and smooth internal business operations. For example, if a guest reports an issue with the cabin temperature to a guest service staff, the staff should immediately report the guest's complaint through management channels to the equipment maintenance department and provide the guest with satisfactory feedback.

（四）信息收集与处理
Information Collection and Processing

前厅是宾客聚集活动的场所,与宾客接触最为频繁。因此,前厅部需随时准备为宾客提供他们所需以及感兴趣的信息资料。例如,邮轮前厅部每日会印发一份《今日活动指南》,涵盖汉语、英语、意大利语、法语、德语、西班牙语、葡萄牙语、俄语、日语等多种语言版本。该指南会在前一天晚上由客舱服务员送至宾客房间,详细列出从清晨到夜晚,各个时间段在不同地点举办的各类活动,像美食制作、艺术展览、电影放映、滑冰表演、毛巾宠物制作课程、手工艺创作、趣味游戏等。这份指南还会注明当天的着装要求,以及船上商店的特价优惠等信息。倘若当天安排了上岸观光活动,指南上也会列出前往岸上观光景点的相关旅游信息。如图1-1所示,即为皇家加勒比邮轮和歌诗达邮轮的每日活动指南。

The front office is a hub of guest activity, having the most frequent contact with guests. Therefore, the guest services department must always be ready to provide guests with information they need and are interested in. For example, the cruise guest services department prints a "Daily Activities Guide" in languages such as Chinese, English, Italian, French, German, Spanish, Portuguese, Russian and Japanese. This guide is delivered to the guests' cabins by the room attendants the night before, detailing the activities taking place from dawn to evening, including the time, location and available activities, such as gourmet cooking classes, art exhibitions, movie screenings, ice skating shows, towel animal folding classes, handicraft making, fun games, etc. The guide also includes dress codes for the day or any special offers at the on board shops. If it's a shore excursion day, the guide will list tourism information about the destinations to be visited. Figure 1-1 shows an example of the daily activities guide from Royal Caribbean Cruises and Costa Cruises.

前厅部还须收集关于客源市场、产品销售、营业收入、宾客意见等方面的信息,对这些信息加以加工、整理,然后将其传递给酒店部的决策管理机构,同时与相关部门做好协调沟通工作。

The guest services department also collects information about the guest source market, product sales, revenue, and guest feedback. It processes this information and passes it on to the decision-making management office of the hotel department, while coordinating and communicating with relevant departments.

（五）管理客账
Guest Account Management

邮轮规定,除赌场消费和支付小费外,其他消费均采用无现金支付系统。宾客登船后,需开通邮轮船卡方可进行消费。前厅部应在宾客登船后,及时协助宾客绑定信用卡或

图 1-1 皇家加勒比邮轮(左)、歌诗达邮轮(右)的《今日活动指南》

Figure 1-1　Daily Activities Guide from Royal Caribbean Cruises and Costa Cruises

收取现金,核算并管理宾客在船上的消费情况,依照规定及时回收账款,以保障邮轮的营业收入,避免出现"漏账"情况。同时,前厅部还负责编制各类会计报表,及时呈现邮轮的经营状况。

On cruise ships, it is required that all expenditures, except for those in casinos and tips, should be made through a cashless payment system. After boarding, guests need to activate their cruise ship cards to make purchases. The guest services department should promptly link the guests' credit cards or collect cash after they board, calculate and manage the guests' on board spending, collect payments timely according to regulations to ensure the cruise's operating income and prevent "missed charges". At the same time, it is responsible for preparing various accounting statements to reflect the cruise's operational status in a timely manner.

(六) 建立宾客历史档案和会员俱乐部管理
Establishment of Guest History Files and Management of the Cruise Membership Club

为了更有效地发挥信息集散与协调服务的职能,前厅部通常会为乘坐邮轮出行超过一次的宾客建立客史档案。在建立客史档案时,一般会将宾客的姓氏、身份、所属公司、出行日期、消费记录以及特殊要求等作为主要内容进行详细记载。这些信息不仅是邮轮为宾客提供周到、细致且具针对性服务的重要依据,也是探寻和分析客源市场、研究市场走势、调整营销策略与产品策略的关键信息来源。

To better play the role of information distribution and coordinating services, the guest services department generally establishes guest history records for guests who have traveled on the cruise more than once. When establishing guest history records, general information such as the guest's surname, identity, company, travel date, consumption record, and special requirements is recorded as the main content. This serves as a basis for the cruise to provide thoughtful, detailed, and targeted services. It is also an important source of information for seeking and analyzing the guest source market, studying market trends, adjusting marketing strategies, and product strategies.

乘坐邮轮出行超过一次的宾客会自动成为邮轮俱乐部会员。宾客出行次数越多,所积累的会员积分就越多,能够享受的优惠折扣与专属特权也就越多、越丰富。会员俱乐部会定期向会员推介邮轮航线、推出会员专属优惠并组织抽奖活动。这不仅能够促进邮轮航线的销售,还有助于维护良好的宾客关系。

Guests who have traveled on the cruise more than once automatically become members of the cruise club. The more trips they take, the more membership points they accumulate, and the more discounts and exclusive privileges they can enjoy. The cruise membership club regularly introduces cruise itineraries to guests, offers member discounts, and organizes lucky draw events, which not only promote the sales of cruise itineraries but also maintain relationships with guests.

任务 2　邮轮前厅部的组织机构
Mission 2
The Organizational Structure of the Cruise Guest Services Department

实训目的
Training Objectives

通过教师对邮轮前厅部组织机构的讲解以及学生对相关资料的阅读分析,学生们将熟悉邮轮前厅部的组织结构,其中涵盖礼宾部、登船部、前台部、总机部、未来航程销售部和岸上观光部等部门。他们将了解到每个部门的职责与功能,以及各部门之间是如何协同运作,从而为宾客提供高效、便捷服务的。学生能够:

Through the teacher's explanation of the organizational structure of the cruise guest services department and students' analysis of related materials, students will become familiar with the organizational setup of the cruise guest services department, including departments such as concierge, boarding, reception, operator, future cruise sales, and shore excursions. They will understand the responsibilities and functions of each department, as well as how they work collaboratively to provide efficient and convenient services to guests. Students will be able to:

1.阐述邮轮前厅部的 6 个主要部门。

Explain the six main departments within the cruise guest services department.

2.区分邮轮前厅部在宾客不同活动周期中的主要工作任务。

Distinguish the main tasks of the cruise guest services department during different guest activity cycles.

3.比较巨型邮轮、大型邮轮、中小型邮轮的前厅部的组织机构的设置差异。
Compare the differences in the organizational setup of the guest services department among very large cruise ships, large cruise ships, small and medium-sized cruise ships.

实训方法 Training Method

首先由教师进行讲解,随后学生对阅读材料展开分析。在小组讨论环节,教师引导学生思考、分析并总结,以达成熟练掌握该学习内容的目标。

First, the teacher will give a lecture, then students analyze the reading materials. During group discussions, the teacher guides students to think, analyze, and summarize, so as to enable students to master the learning content proficiently.

实训准备 Training Preparation

阅读资料1:快捷高效的登船手续。
Reading Material 1: Efficient Boarding Procedures.

实训内容及操作标准 Training Content and Operating Stardards

合理的组织机构与明确的岗位职责,是确保组织正常运转的前提条件。就邮轮前厅部而言,其组织机构的设置需要综合考量邮轮的吨位、目标市场、接待特点以及管理方式等诸多因素,以避免机构出现重叠与臃肿的情况。与此同时,各部门之间应当做到任务清晰、分工明确且协同合作,并接受统一指挥。

A reasonable organizational structure and clear job responsibilities are the preconditions for ensuring the normal operation of an organization. For the cruise guest services department, the setup of its organizational structure should be comprehensively considered in terms of factors such as the cruise ship's tonnage, target market, reception characteristics, and management style, to avoid overlapping and bloated departments. At the same time, there should be clear tasks, division of labor, collaboration, and unified command among all departments.

阅读资料1(Material 1):

快捷高效的登船手续
Efficient Boarding Procedures

来自上海的苏女士在某旅游论坛上,与大家分享了她的歌诗达邮轮之旅,尤其对歌诗达邮轮快捷高效的登船流程安排赞不绝口:

Mrs. Su from Shanghai shared her Costa Cruise journey on a travel forum, particularly praising the efficient boarding process arranged by Costa Cruises:

"一到达港口,歌诗达邮轮公司的工作人员就在港口迎接我们,引导我们前往行李集中区,发给我们歌诗达专用的行李牌。他们提醒我们,大件行李必须托运,小件行李可以随身携带,护照、身份证以及贵重物品等也需要随身携带。我们把房号写在行李牌上,然后系到行李上,最后交给工作人员,整个过程前后一共耗时1分钟。邮轮公司的工作人员说,我们的行李会由行李生直接送至客舱。"

"Upon arriving at the port, we were greeted by staff from Costa Cruises who guided us to the luggage collection area, handed out Costa's exclusive luggage tags, reminded us that large bags had to be checked in while small bags could be carried on board, along with passports, IDs, and valuables. We wrote our cabin numbers on the luggage tags, attached them to our bags, and handed them over to the staff, which took only 1 minute. The cruise staff mentioned that our luggage would be delivered directly to our cabins by the bellboys."

"办理完行李托运后,我们依照登船指示牌的提示,前往登记柜台办理登船手续。我们出示了护照、护照复印件以及船票,很快就领到了印有个人信息的邮轮船卡。工作人员询问我们是否需要一并关联信用卡,得知仅需半分钟就能完成关联,我们果断拿出信用卡,填好信用授权单,果不其然,不到半分钟就关联好了。"

"After checking in our luggage, we followed the boarding signs to the registration counter to complete the boarding procedures, presenting our passports, passport copies, and cruise tickets. Soon, we received our personalized cruise cards. The staff asked if we wanted to link our credit cards, and hearing it would only take half a minute, we decisively took out our credit cards, filled out the credit authorization form, and indeed, the linking was completed in less than half a minute."

"拿着船卡,我们顺利通过了安检与海关,沿着廊桥登上了期盼已久的'歌诗达大西洋号'邮轮,就此开启了我们的东南亚之旅。"

"Holding our cruise cards, we smoothly passed through security checks and customs, and embarked on the much-anticipated Costa Atlantica via the gangway, and then started our journey to Southeast Asia."

登船部是邮轮前厅部极为关键的一个部门。每当邮轮停靠港口,便是登船部员工最为忙碌之际。此时,往往需要其他部门员工全力协作,才能完成数千名宾客同时进行的登船与下船手续办理工作。

The boarding department is an extremely crucial section of the cruise guest services department. Whenever the cruise docks at a port, the boarding department staff are at their busiest. At this time, the cooperation of staff from other departments is often required to complete the simultaneous boarding and disembarkation procedures for thousands of people.

一、邮轮前厅部部门设置
Departmental Setup of the Cruise Guest Services Department

（一）邮轮前厅部主要部门
Main Departments of the Cruise Guest Services Department

关于邮轮前厅部的部门设置，不同的邮轮公司存在差异。一般而言，邮轮前厅部由前台、总机、礼宾、登船等部门构成。部分邮轮公司，比如维京邮轮，还将岸上观光和未来航程销售业务也纳入邮轮前厅部的职能范畴内。邮轮前厅部的主要部门设置情况如图1-2所示。

Regarding the departmental setup of the cruise guest services department, different cruise companies have their own variations. Generally speaking, the cruise guest services department is composed of departments such as the Front Desk, Operator, Concierge, and Boarding, etc. Some cruise companies, like Viking Cruises, also include shore excursions and future cruise sales within the cruise guest services department. The main departmental setup of the cruise guest services department is illustrated in Figure 1-2.

图1-2 邮轮前厅部部门设置
Figure 1-2 Department Setup of the Cruise Guest Services Department

1. 前台部（Front Desk Department/Reception Department）

前台部，又称为接待处，主要负责接待宾客，为宾客提供服务并解决问题。该部门是邮轮前厅部的核心部门，通常设置在大堂甲板十分显眼的位置，便于宾客寻找与抵达。前台设有前台经理、宾客关系经理、接待员以及国际翻译专员等职位。其主要职责包括：推销客房；为宾客提供舱房更换与升舱服务；提供咨询解答服务；编制邮轮简报；进行收银结账服务；开展外币兑换业务；提供物品租借服务；接待来访宾客；处理宾客邮件、留言并进行分发；处理和解决宾客投诉；维护宾客关系等。

The front desk department, also known as reception department, is primarily responsible for greeting guests and providing services and solving their problems. This department is the core of the cruise guest services department, usually located in a very visible area of the lobby deck for easy access of guests. The front desk is staffed with positions such as front desk manager, guest relations manager, receptionists, and international interpreters. Its main responsibilities include: selling cabins; providing guests with cabin changes and upgrades; offering consultation and answering services; producing cruise briefings; conducting cashier and check-out services; foreign currency exchange; item lending; receiving visiting guests; handling guest mail, messages, and distribution; dealing with and resolving guest complaints; and maintaining guest relations, etc.

2.总机部 (Operator Department)

总机部配备有总机主管(领班)和话务员。其主要职责是转接邮轮与陆地之间的电话,回应宾客通过电话提出的询问,提供电话找人、电话投诉受理、留言转达服务以及叫醒服务等。

The operator department is equipped with an operator supervisor (team leader) and operators, mainly responsible for connecting calls between the cruise and land, answering guest phone inquiries, providing paging service by phone, handling phone complaints, message relay services, wake-up calls, etc.

3.礼宾部 (Concierge Department)

礼宾部,也称作套房礼宾关系部,主要面向套房宾客与VIP宾客提供贵宾接待服务以及各类委托代办服务,同时也为邮轮上的全体宾客提供行李搬运服务。礼宾部主要由礼宾主管、礼宾关系专员、贴身管家、行李员等人员构成。其主要职责涵盖:在港口迎接套房宾客和VIP宾客;为宾客提供行李托运服务;引领宾客前往客房;协助宾客预订船上的娱乐项目及餐饮服务;解答宾客的咨询,为宾客指引方向;代办宾客委托的各项事务等。

The concierge department, also known as suite concierge relations, primarily provides VIP reception services and various commissioned services for suite guests and VIP guests, as well as luggage carrying services for all cruise guests. The concierge department is mainly composed of a concierge supervisor, concierge relations specialists, butlers, bellmen, and other personnel. Its main responsibilities include: greeting suite guests and VIP guests at the port; providing guests with luggage check-in services; escorting guests to their rooms; assisting guests with on board entertainment and dining reservations; answering guest inquiries and guiding guests; handling various commissioned affairs for guests, among others.

4.登船部 (Boarding Department)

登船部主要设有登船专员、离船专员、行政专员等岗位。其主要职责是处理与宾客上下船相关的事务,例如与海关、港口进行沟通,确定邮轮的停靠时间以及宾客上下船的时间等;同时,该部门还负责保管宾客的护照、签证等相关证件。

The boarding department is mainly staffed with boarding specialists, disembarkation specialists, administrative specialists, etc., primarily responsible for matters related to guests boarding and disembarking, such as communicating with customs and ports about the cruise's docking time and guests' boarding and disembarking times, while also being responsible for safekeeping guests' passports, visas, and other relevant documents.

5. 岸上观光（Shore Excursion）

目前,许多邮轮会在邮轮前台附近设立岸上观光服务台,该服务台隶属于邮轮前厅部。此部门设有岸上观光预订员、导游、团队协调员等岗位。其主要职责包括:为宾客设计并预订岸上观光路线;提供陆地导游服务;负责与邮轮中间商、代理商进行沟通和协调等工作。

Currently, many cruise companies set up a shore excursion service desk near the cruise reception desk, which falls under the cruise guest services department. This department includes positions such as shore excursion reservationists, tour guides, team coordinators, etc. Its main responsibilities are to design and book shore excursion itineraries for guests; provide land guiding services; communicate and coordinate with cruise intermediaries and agents, among others.

6. 未来航程销售（Future Cruise Sales）

鉴于未来航程销售对于邮轮运营的重要性,多数邮轮公司会在邮轮前台附近设立未来航程销售服务台,该服务台配备有未来航程销售经理及销售员。其主要职责是面向船上宾客开展未来航程的销售工作,通过提供优惠举措,推动宾客进行预订。总的来说,这是一项针对常客推出的忠诚宾客优惠项目。

Due to the importance of future cruise sales to the cruise companies, most cruise companies set up a future cruise sales service desk near the cruise reception desk, staffed with a future cruise sales manager and salespeople. Its main responsibility is to sell future cruises to guests on board, offering promotional measures to encourage bookings. In summary, it is a loyalty program for regular guests.

(二) 邮轮前厅部在宾客各个活动周期中的主要工作任务
The Main Tasks of the Cruise Guest Services Department Throughout the Guest's Activity Cycle

借鉴宾客在酒店的4个活动周期,我们也将宾客在邮轮上的活动周期划分为4个阶段:乘船之前、登船之际、乘船期间、下船之际,如图1-3所示。

Drawing from the four activity cycles of hotel guests, we also divide the activity cycle of cruise guests into four stages: before boarding, boarding, on the cruise, and disembarking, as shown in Figure 1-3.

邮轮前厅部在宾客上述4个活动周期中发挥着至关重要的作用,其主要工作任务包括:推销客房并完成舱房预订、提供优质的接待服务、为宾客提供各类综合服务以及负责客舱账务处理等。邮轮前厅部在宾客各活动周期中的主要工作任务详见表1-1。

The cruise guest services department plays a pivotal role in the above four activity cycles of guests, with its main tasks including: selling cabins and handling cabin reservations, providing high-quality reception services, offering various comprehensive services to guests, and managing cabin accounting. The main work tasks of the cruise guest services department during each guest activity cycle are shown in Table 1-1.

模块1　邮轮前厅部概要
Module 1　Introduction: the Cruise Guest Services Department

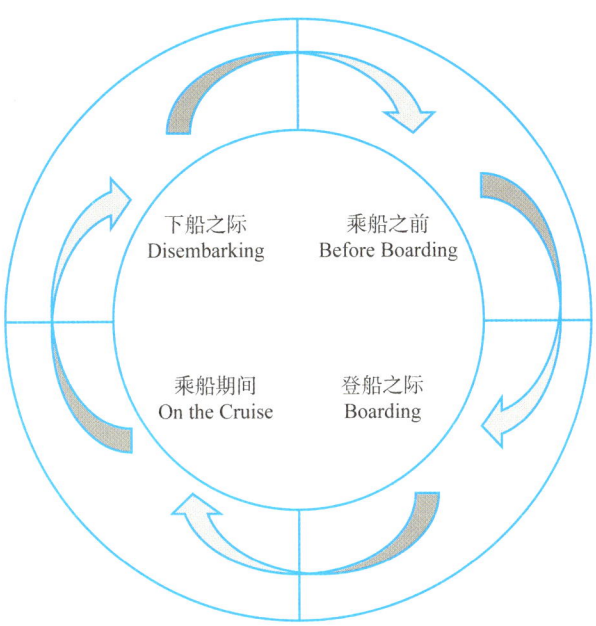

图 1-3　宾客在邮轮上的活动周期
Figure 1-3　The Activity Cycle of Cruise Guests

表 1-1　邮轮前厅部在宾客各活动周期中的主要工作任务
Table 1-1　The Main Work Tasks of the Cruise Guest Services Department During Each guest Activity Cycle

阶　段 Stage	任　务 Tasks	岗　位 Positions
第一阶段 First Stage	客房推销和预订 Room Promotion and Reservation	岸上销售/未来航程销售 Onshore Sales/Future Cruise Sales
第二阶段 Second Stage	行李托运 Luggage Check-in	礼宾部 Concierge Department
	办理上船登记 Check-in	登船部 Boarding Department
	分发邮轮船卡 Distribution of Cruise Cards	
	证件收取和管理 Documents Collection and Management	
	套房宾客和VIP宾客接待 Reception for Suite Guests and VIP Guests	礼宾部 Concierge Department

续表

阶 段 Stage	任 务 Tasks	岗 位 Positions
第三阶段 Third Stage	外币兑换和账务管理 Foreign Currency Exchange and Account Management	前台部 Reception Department
	舱房更换和升舱 Cabin Change and Upgrade	
	问讯、邮件、物品租借 Inquiries, Mail, Item Rental	
	投诉受理和解决 Complaint Reception and Resolution	
	未来航程推销 Future Cruise Marketing	未来航程销售 Future Cruise Sales
	电话转接 Phone Transfer	总机部 Operator Department
	岸上观光预订和导游服务 Shore Excursion Reservation and Tour Guide Services	岸上观光 Shore Excursion
	停靠港和上下船 Boarding and Departure at Ports	登船部 Boarding Department
	船上娱乐及餐饮预订等委托代办服务 Commissioned Services (e.g. Entertainment and Dining Reservations) on Board	礼宾部 Concierge Department
第四阶段 Fourth Stage	行李托运 Luggage Check-in	礼宾部 Concierge Department
	收银结账 Cashier and Check-out	前台部 Reception Department
	办理下船 Disembarkation	登船部 Boarding Department

二、邮轮前厅部组织机构图
Organizational Chart of the Cruise Guest Services Department

（一）巨型邮轮前厅部组织机构
Organizational Structure of the Cruise Guest Services Department on Very Large Cruise Ships

巨型邮轮通常是指吨位在 7 万吨及以上的邮轮。这类邮轮的前厅部组织机构完善，分工细致合理，层级架构清晰。其分设了前台部、总机部、登船部和礼宾部等面向宾客的服务部门，并设有部门经理、主管、领班和服务员四个职务层级。如图 1-4 所示，展示的是常见的巨型邮轮前厅部组织机构示意图。

Very Large Cruise Ships generally refer to cruise ships with a tonnage of 70,000 tons or more. Their guest services department have a complete organizational structure, clear division of labor, and distinct hierarchical levels. They are divided into guest service departments such as the reception department, operator department, boarding department and concierge department. There are four hierarchical levels: manager, supervisor, team leader, and attendant. As shown in Figure1-4, it is a common organizational structure chart of the cruise guest services department on Very Large Cruise Ships.

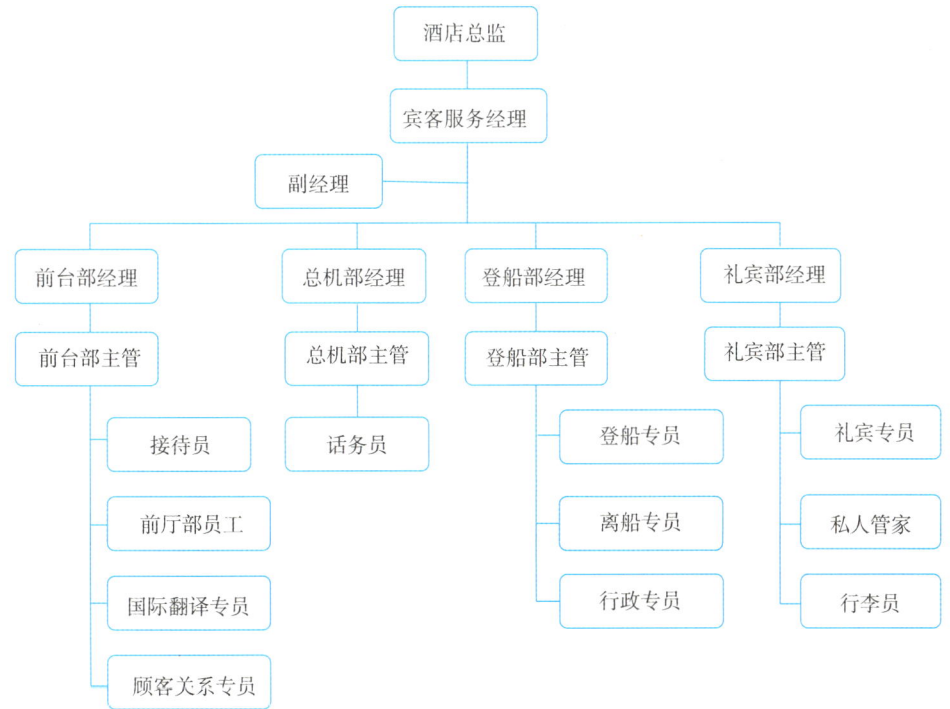

图1-4 巨型邮轮前厅部组织机构

（二）大型邮轮前厅部组织机构
Organizational Structure of the Cruise Guest Services Department on Large Cruise Ships

大型邮轮通常是指吨位处于5万吨以上至7万吨以下区间的邮轮。相较于巨型邮轮,大型邮轮的前厅部机构构成有所精简,设置了前台部、登船部以及礼宾部等面向宾客的服务岗位。尽管机构有所减少,但职能依然完备,能够充分满足接待服务的各项需求。其管理层级也相应减少,一般设有部门经理、主管(或领班)以及服务员这三个层级。如图1-5所示,展示的是常见的大型邮轮前厅部组织机构示意图。

Large Cruise Ships refer to those with a tonnage between more than 50,000 and less than 70,000 tons. Compared to Very Large Cruise Ships, the front office department on large cruise ships has a reduced organizational structure, equipped with guest service positions such as the reception department, boarding department, and concierge department. While the num-

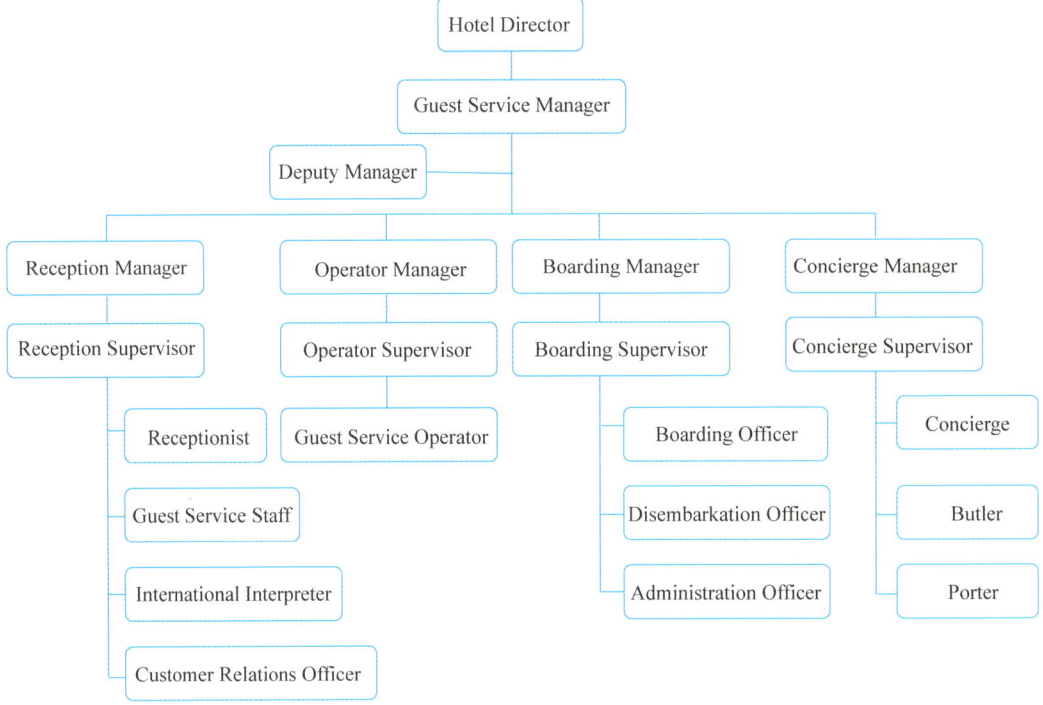

Figure1-4　Organizational Structure of the Cruise Guest Services Department on Very Large Cruise Ships

ber of departments has decreased, its functions remain complete and can fully meet the needs of reception services. The management hierarchy is streamlined, generally consisting of three levels: department manager, supervisor (or team leader), and service staff. As shown in Figure1-5, it illustrates a common organizational structure chart of the cruise guest services department on a Large Cruise Ship.

中小型邮轮前厅部组织机构
Organizational Structure of the Cruise Guest Services Department on Small and Medium-sized Cruise Ships

吨位在5万吨以下的邮轮被称作中小型邮轮。在中小型邮轮上,一般在酒店总监之下设置前台部经理一职,该经理负责统筹接待、问询、收银、总机、登船、离船以及礼宾等一系列面向宾客的服务工作。其组织架构通常仅设有领班和服务员两个层级。如图1-6所示,展示的是常见的中小型邮轮前厅部组织机构示意图。

Cruise ships with a tonnage of less than 50,000 tons are referred to as Small and Medium-sized Cruise Ships. Generally, under the hotel director, there is a front office manager responsible for guest services such as reception, inquiry, cashiering, telephone operator, boarding, disembarkation, and concierge. Usually, there are only two hierarchical levels: team leader and service staff. As shown in Figure1-6, it illustrates a common organizational structure of the cruise guest services department on Small and Medium-sized Cruise Ships.

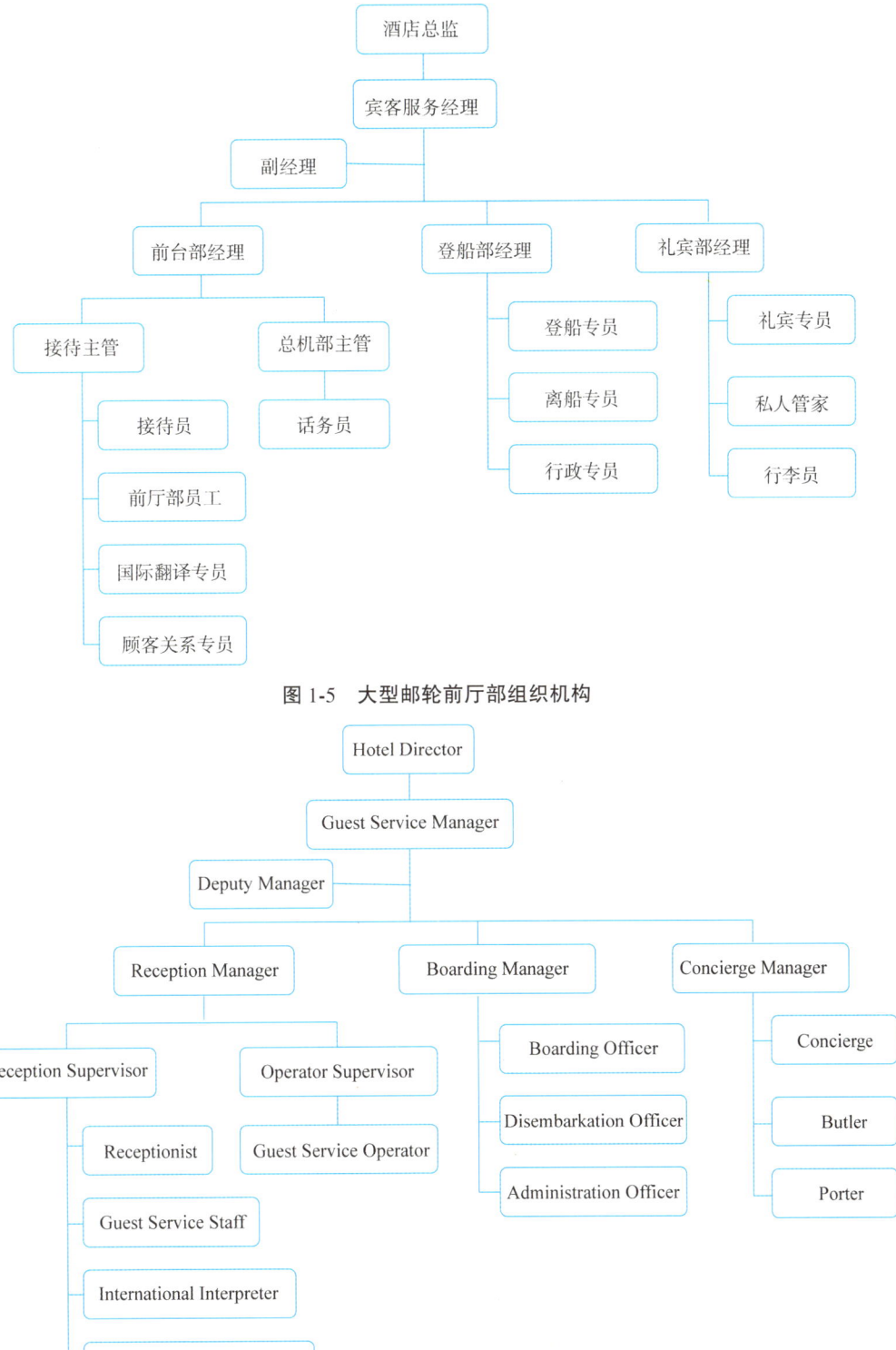

图1-5 大型邮轮前厅部组织机构

Figure1-5　Organizational Structure of the Cruise Guest Services Department on Large Cruise Ships

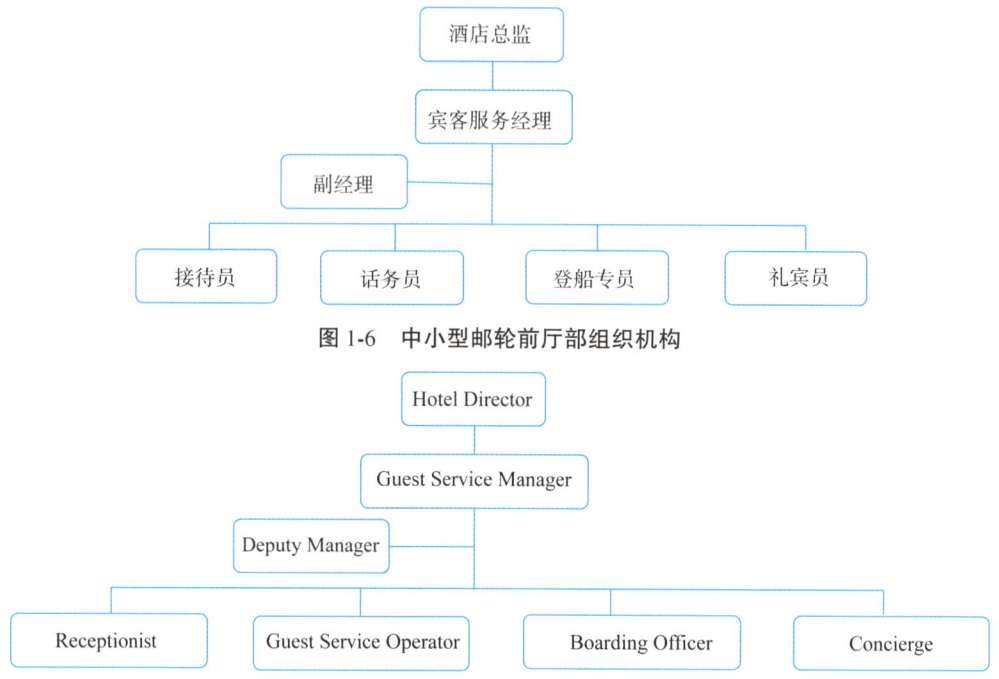

图 1-6 中小型邮轮前厅部组织机构

Figure1-6 Organizational Structure of the Cruise Guest Services Department on Small and Medium-sized Cruise Ships

任务3 邮轮前厅部员工的素质要求
Mission 3
The Quality Requirements for the Cruise Guest Service Staff

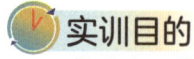

实训目的
Training Objectives

通过教师对邮轮前厅部员工工作内容的分享以及案例分析，学生们将能够深入理解邮轮前厅部的工作性质、职责以及所面临的挑战。以下是学生们可能从这一教学过程中获得的具体知识和技能：

Through the teacher's sharing of the work content of the cruise guest service staff and case analysis, students will be able to gain an in-depth understanding of the nature of work, responsibilities, and challenges faced by the cruise guest services department. The specific knowledge and skills that students may acquire from this teaching process include the ability to:

1.阐述员工端庄的仪容仪表的3个层次的含义。
State the three levels of meaning behind the decent appearance and demeanor of employees.
2.演示展现得体的站姿、坐姿、走姿与蹲姿。
Demonstrate appropriate standing, sitting, walking, and squatting postures.
3.区别海上的生活与陆地上的生活的差别。
Tell the differences between the life at sea and the life on land.

实训方法
Training Method

首先,由教师进行讲解和示范,随后学生分组开展演练并分析案例材料。在学生进行操作训练时,教师予以指导,学生通过反复强化训练,以熟练掌握该项操作技能。在小组讨论环节,教师引导学生进行思考、分析与总结,助力学生熟练掌握相关学习内容。

The lesson begins with the teacher's explanations and demonstrations, followed by students in groups practicing and analyzing case studies. During students' operation training, the teacher provides guidance, allowing students to repeatedly reinforce their training to master the operation skill proficiently. In group discussions, the teacher guides students to think, analyze, and summarize, helping students master the relevant learning content.

实训准备
Training Preparation

阅读资料1:美国公主邮轮招聘简章
Reading Material 1: Recruitment Brochure of Princess Cruises in the USA
阅读资料2:迪士尼邮轮的形象要求
Reading Material 2: Image Requirements for Disney Cruises
阅读资料3:海上生活剪影
Reading Material 3: Snapshots of Life at Sea
椅子等。
Chairs, etc.

实训内容及操作标准
Training Content and Operating Stardards

阅读资料1(Material 1):

美国公主邮轮招聘简章
Recruitment Brochure of Princess Cruises in the USA

一、关于公主邮轮
About Princess Cruises

美国公主邮轮公司创立于1965年,是全球规模最大、服务品质最佳的邮轮公司之一,旗下拥有17艘吨位超过10万吨的豪华邮轮。其航线覆盖全球200多个风景秀丽的知名港口。公主邮轮是当今世界上一家将餐饮、娱乐以及名胜游览融为一体,并为宾客提供多样化灵活选择的高端邮轮公司。

Princess Cruises, founded in 1965, is one of the largest and best-serviced cruise companies worldwide, owning 17 luxury cruise ships each weighing over 100,000 tons. Its itineraries cover more than 200 picturesque and well-known ports globally. Princess Cruises is currently a premier cruise company that integrates dining, entertainment, and sightseeing, providing flexible options for guests.

二、岗位及待遇(工资以美金结算,每两周一次)

Positions and Compensation (Wages are settled in US dollars, bi-weekly)

前厅部

Cruise Guest Services Department

客服经理

Guest Service Manager

前厅部员工

Guest Service Staff

岸上观光经理

Shore Excursions Manager

导游

Tour Guide

国际翻译专员

International Interpreter

证件管理专员

Assistant Purser/Administrative Specialist

以上岗位,根据职位的不同,综合收入 = 底薪 + 小费 + 服务费,约为600至4000美元。员工可享受免费的食宿待遇,住宿一般为两人一间(房间内配备有卫生间、电视、储物柜等设施),同时还提供免费医疗服务(牙齿治疗除外)以及船员保险。

The comprehensive income of the above positions, which varies according to different positions, is composed of base salary + tips + service fee, approximately between 600 and 4000 USD. Employees can enjoy free meals and accommodation generally, there are two people sharing one room, (which is equipped with a bathroom, TV, locker, etc.). Meanwhile, free medical care (excluding dental treatment) and crew insurance are also provided.

三、工作时间及合同期

Working Hours and Contract Period

每天工作时长约为10至13小时(含工作餐及工间咖啡休息时间,实行责任制工作)。邮轮靠岸后,未值班的邮轮乘务员可以上岸购物或游玩。合同期通常为6至10个月,一个合同期结束后,员工回国休假2个月。后续若双方意愿一致,可续签合同,且均按照国际海员法相关条例签订劳工合同。

Work approximately 10 to 13 hours daily (including meal and coffee breaks, with a responsibility-based work system). When the cruise ship is docked, off-duty crew members may go ashore for shopping and sightseeing. The contract period ranges from 6 to 10 months. After one contract period ends, employees will have a 2-month vacation back in their home country. Subsequent contract renewals will be carried out if both parties agree, and all labor contracts will be signed in accordance with international maritime laws and regulations.

四、要求

Requirements

招聘要求如下：性别不限，年龄需在21岁及以上。需具备英语交流能力，掌握邮轮、酒店行业专业技能，或拥有相关工作经验。身体健康（无传染病史）。具备良好的服务意识，能够适应全英语的工作环境，能够与来自世界各地的同事友好协作。能吃苦耐劳，遵守法律法规，无任何不良记录。

The recruitment requirements are as follows: gender is not restricted, candidates must be over 21 years old, and able to communicate in English, possess professional skills in the cruise or hotel industry or have relevant work experience, be in good health (free from contagious diseases), have a good sense of service, be able to adapt to an all-English working environment, cooperate amicably with colleagues from around the globe, be hardworking and law-abiding, with no negative records.

讨论：邮轮前厅部员工应该具备哪些素质要求？

Discussion: What qualities should cruise guest service staff possess?

阅读资料2（Material 2）：

迪士尼邮轮的形象要求
Image Requirements for Disney Cruises

作为一名船员，你应当维护我们全球闻名的友好且经典的形象。迪士尼员工的形象源于迪士尼的理念，即每一位船员在引领宾客进入梦幻世界的过程中都扮演着重要角色。依据我们的指导原则，你和你的团队要展现出专业的"舞台"形象，彰显迪士尼品牌，提升整体宾客体验，维护品牌"形象"。

As a crew member, you should maintain our globally renowned friendly and classic image. The Disney employee image is derived from the Disney philosophy that each crew member plays an important role in guiding guests into a magical world. Following our guidelines, you and your team will present a professional "on-stage" image, representing the Disney brand and enhancing the overall guest experience and the brand "image".

女性形象要求如下：

Female appearance requirements are as follows:

(1) 头发必须梳理整齐，发型应偏向保守经典风格。

Hair must be neatly groomed and hairstyles should lean towards conservative and classic styles.

(2) 发饰要简约素净，以纯色为主，且需与服装搭配协调。

Hair accessories should be plain, mainly in solid colors, and be in harmony with the clothing.

(3)需化淡妆,妆容色调应与肤色适配。

Wear light makeup that complements the skin tone.

(4)指甲油颜色要与肤色相衬,不可选用亮色,也禁止贴花。

Nail polish should match the skin tone and must not be in bright colors nor have decals.

(5)所戴饰品应具备简约、精致、小巧的特点。

Jewelry should feature simplicity, delicacy, and smallness.

(6)严禁戴有色眼镜,要确保眼睛能被宾客看到,以自然眼眸颜色与宾客进行眼神交流。

Colored glasses are strictly prohibited to ensure that guests can see your eyes, and make eye contact with them using the natural eye color.

(7)名牌应始终佩戴于左胸上方位置。

Name tags should always be worn above the left chest.

(8)工服需时刻保持干净、整洁。

Work uniforms should always be kept clean and tidy.

(9)工作期间,文身和/或刺青穿孔等不得外露。

Tattoos and/or piercings must not be exposed during work.

男性员工的形象要求如下:

Male employee appearance requirements are as follows:

(1)头发必须修剪整齐,两侧不得遮住耳朵,后部不得盖住衣领。

Hair must be neatly trimmed. It should not cover the ears on the sides or the collar at the back.

(2)应选用自然色系的护发产品。

Naturally-colored hair products should be used.

(3)头发颜色务必自然,禁止烫染夸张色彩。

Hair color must be natural, and the use of exaggerated dyed colors is prohibited.

(4)面部毛发(胡须等)必须修剪整齐,风格偏向保守。

Facial hair (such as beards, etc.) must be neatly trimmed and should be in a conservative style.

(5)饰品方面,每只手仅可戴一枚戒指,此外还可戴一块商务风格的手表。

Regarding jewelry, only one ring is allowed on each hand, and a business-style watch is also permitted.

(6)严禁戴有色眼镜,要确保眼睛能被宾客看到,以自然眼眸颜色与宾客进行眼神交流。

Colored glasses are strictly prohibited to ensure that the eyes are visible to guests, and make eye contact with them using the natural eye color.

(7)名牌应始终佩戴于左胸上方位置。

Name tags should always be worn above the left chest.

(8)工服需时刻保持干净、整洁。

Work uniforms should always be kept clean and tidy.

(9)工作期间,文身和/或刺青穿孔等不得外露。

Tattoos and/or piercings must not be exposed during work.

由于工作环境的特殊性,邮轮服务人员除了要掌握扎实的专业知识、具备娴熟的职业技能外,还需达到更高的素质要求。

Due to the unique nature of the working environment, in addition to possessing solid professional knowledge and professional skills, cruise service staff need to meet higher qualitative requirements.

一、良好的外部形象
Good External Image

前厅是宾客聚集与疏散的场所,前厅部员工代表着整艘邮轮迎接每一位宾客。高大挺拔的身材、良好的外在形象,能够让宾客在心理上获得愉悦之感,给宾客留下美好的印象。这里所说的外在形象,既涵盖外貌、仪容,也包含仪表、仪态以及举止等方面。举止是展现个人才华与修养的重要外在表现形式,得体的举止有助于一个人迈向成功。

The Reception is a place where guests gather and disperse, and the guest service staff represent the entire cruise ship in greeting every guest. A tall and upright stature and good appearance can bring guests a sense of delight, leaving them with a favorable impression. The appearance here includes not only looks and personal grooming but also manner, appearance and behavior. Behavior is an important external manifestation of one's talents and cultivation; appropriate behavior can help a person achieve success.

(一) 端庄的仪容仪表
Decent and Generous Grooming and Appearance

仪表,即人的外在表象,一般而言,涵盖人的容貌、服饰、个人卫生以及姿态等多个方面。仪容主要聚焦于人的面部容貌,是仪表至关重要的构成部分。端庄大方的仪容仪表是一个综合性概念,它包含三个层面的内涵:其一,指人的容貌、身形与仪态相互协调而呈现出的优美状态;其二,指经修饰装扮后,结合后天所处环境影响所塑造出的美感;其三,指内在美自然而然的一种外在流露。

Appearance refers to a person's looks, generally including aspects such as looks, clothing, personal hygiene, and posture. Grooming mainly refers to a person's facial features, which is an important part of appearance. A dignified and elegant appearance and grooming is a comprehensive concept, encompassing three levels of meaning: Firstly, it refers to the harmonious and beautiful coordination of a person's looks, body, and demeanor; Secondly, it refers to the beauty formed after adornment and the influence of the acquired environment; Thirdly, it refers to a natural display of inner beauty.

1. 头发(Hair)

禁止漂染艳丽发色,禁止烫发。要坚持勤洗头发,定期修剪并经常梳理,保持头发干净整齐。男性员工头发长度标准为后部不盖住衣领、两侧不遮挡耳朵;可以使用发胶,但头发不可显得过于油腻或湿塌。女性员工前刘海不可超过眉毛,鬓发不能盖住耳部,头发不得触及后衣领,过肩长发必须束起,不得戴色彩艳丽的饰品。

Bleaching or dying hair in bright colors and perming are prohibited. Hair should be washed frequently, trimmed regularly, combed often to maintain cleanliness and neatness. Male employees' hair should not cover the collar at the back or the ears on the sides; hair gel can be used, but the hair should not appear too greasy or wet. Female employees' bangs should not cover the eyebrows, sideburns should not cover the ears, hair should not touch the back collar. Long hair over the shoulders must be tied up and colorful decorations are not allowed.

2.面容(Facial Features)

需注重清洁与适度修饰,以保持容光焕发的状态。应确保皮肤处于不油腻、不干燥且无皮屑的良好状态,严禁戴有色眼镜。男性员工需时常留意并修剪鼻毛,防止鼻毛外露。女性员工可适度化妆,不过应以淡雅妆容为佳,杜绝浓妆艳抹,同时避免使用气味浓烈的化妆品。

One should pay attention to cleanliness and appropriate grooming to maintain a radiant complexion. Skin should be neither oily nor dry, without dandruff, and wearing colored glasses is strictly prohibited. Male employees should pay attention to and trim nose hairs to prevent nose hairs from being exposed. Female employees may apply makeup moderately, yet heavy or garish makeup, as well as cosmetics with strong scents, should be avoided.

3.手部(Hands)

要经常洗手,确保手部,尤其是指甲保持洁净;需定期修剪指甲,使其长度适中。男性员工应保持手部清洁,不能有因吸烟而残留的污渍,指甲长度以刚能覆盖指尖为宜,且不可涂抹指甲油。女性员工禁止涂有色指甲油。

One should wash hands frequently to keep hands, especially fingernails, clean; nails should be trimmed to an appropriate length. Male employees should keep their hands clean, without smoking-related stains, with nails covering only the fingertips, and not use nail polish. Female employees should not apply colored nail polish.

4.着装(Dress)

需穿着公司规定的制服,确保制服整齐、干净、平整、大方、美观且合身。穿着衬衫时,需将其束进长裤或裙子内,长袖衬衫的袖口不可卷起,袖口的纽扣要扣好。注意:内衣不得外露,不得掉扣、漏扣,不可挽起衣袖、卷起裤脚;领带、领结或飘带与衬衫领口要贴合紧密且不能系歪;姓名牌应佩戴在左胸正上方位置。需穿着黑色皮鞋或布鞋,皮鞋要擦拭得光亮,无破损,搭配深色且无鲜艳花纹的袜子,同时要勤加换洗,保持袜子无异味。

Wear the company-prescribed uniform, ensuring it is neat, clean, crisp, elegant, attractive, and appropriate. Shirts must be tucked into trousers or skirts; sleeve cuffs should not be rolled up, and cuff buttons should be fastened. Note: Undergarments must not be visible. Buttons must not be missing or loose, and sleeves and trouser legs must not be rolled up. Ties, bow ties, and streamers should fit snugly against the shirt collar without being crooked; name tags should be worn directly above the left chest. Wear black leather or fabric shoes, which should be polished and undamaged, with dark socks without bright patterns. Wash and change the socks frequently to avoid odors.

5.饰品(Jewelry)

前厅部员工所戴的饰品应当符合岗位要求,且工艺精湛。前厅部员工可以戴一枚款式简约的戒指,并且要戴在正确位置。女性员工可以戴耳钉或者长度不超过耳垂的耳环,此外,还可戴质地轻盈、体积小巧、做工精致的金项链或银项链。

Guest service staff should wear jewelry that meets job requirements and is well-made. The guest service staff may wear one simply-designed ring and position it correctly. Female employees may wear stud earrings or earrings, but the length should not exceed the earlobe, and they may also wear a light, small, and refined gold or silver necklace.

(二) 优雅得体的仪态举止
Elegant and Appropriate Posture and Demeanor

仪态指的是人在行为活动中的姿势与风度。姿势即身体所呈现出的各类形态;风度则体现为人的举止动作以及待人接物时展现出的外在表现形式,属于气质层面的自然流露。风度美是一种综合性、完备性的美,这种美应当是身体各部位器官相互协调配合的整体呈现,同时也涵盖了一个人内在素养与外在仪态之间的和谐统一。

Bearing refers to the posture and demeanor of a person during behavioral activities. Posture refers to the various forms the body takes, while demeanor is a person's way of behaving and interacting with others, an external manifestation that reflects one's temperament. The beauty of demeanor is a comprehensive and consummate beauty, encompassing the harmonious coordination of all parts of the body, as well as the harmony between a person's inner qualities and their bearing.

在前厅接待工作中,要求服务人员展现出端庄稳重、落落大方的仪态风度。端庄体现于服务人员的整体形象,大方则是服务人员应具备的特有风度。唯有热情和蔼、大方得体地为宾客提供服务,方能赢得宾客的信任,吸引更多宾客。

In guest service reception, service staff are required to maintain a dignified and composed, generous and natural demeanor. Dignity represents the image of the service staff, while generosity is the demeanor they should possess. Only by serving guests warmly, kindly, and appropriately can service staff earn the trust of guests and attract more guests.

1.站姿(Standing Posture)

前厅部员工站立时,头部需端正,双目平视前方,嘴唇微微闭合,下颌微微内收,保持面容平和自然。双肩放松,略向下沉,让身体呈现向上的挺拔感。躯干要挺直,切实做到挺胸、收腹、立腰。双手自然下垂于身体两侧,中指轻轻贴靠裤缝。双腿应笔直站立、并拢,脚跟相互靠拢,双脚呈60°夹角。

When standing, guest service staff should keep their head straight, eyes level, lips slightly closed, jaw slightly retracted, face calm and natural, shoulders relaxed and slightly drooped, making the body appear upright and uplifted, torso straight, chest expanded, abdomen drawn in, and waist kept straight, with hands naturally hanging by the body sides, middle fingers gently touching the trouser seams, legs straight and together, heels touching, feet forming a 60° angle.

此外,男女站立姿势存在差异:男士站立时,应保持身体挺直,右手搭于左手上,轻贴于臀部位置,双腿微微分开,双脚平行,间距与肩同宽或稍宽一些;女士站立时,需保持身体笔直,双臂自然下垂,右手搭在左手上,贴合于腹部,双腿并拢,脚跟紧密相靠,双脚可前后略微分开,或分开呈"V"字形,抑或是呈"T"字形(如图1-7所示)。

Additionally, the standing posture differs between men and women: men should stand with their body straight, the right hand placed on the left hand and resting on the hip, legs apart, feet parallel, at shoulder-width or slightly wider; women should stand with their body straight, arms hanging down, the right hand placed on the left hand and resting on the abdomen, legs together, heels close, feet slightly apart, with one foot in front of the other or forming a "V" shape or "T" shape (Figure 1-7).

(a) 女士站姿　　　　　　(b) 男士站姿
Female Standing Posture　　Male Standing Posture

图 1-7　站姿
Figure 1-7　Standing Posture

特别需要注意的是,前厅部员工站立时切勿过于随意,不可出现探脖、塌腰、耸肩、双腿弯曲或不停抖动等情况。在庄重场合,双手切勿放入衣兜或叉在腰间,这些不良站姿会给他人留下负面印象。在非正式场合,若感到疲惫,可适度调整姿态,例如:将一条腿向前跨出半步,或者向后撤半步,让身体重心在两条腿上交替转移。倘若这些姿态运用得当,不仅能缓解疲劳,还不会有损风度美。

It's particularly important to note that guest service staff should not stand too casually, avoid stretching necks, slouching, shrugging, having bent legs or constantly jiggling one's legs. In solemn occasions, hands should not be put in pockets or placed on the hips, as these postures leave a bad impression. In informal situations, if tired, one can slightly adjust posture, for example: taking half a step forward or backward with one leg, alternating the body's center of gravity between the two legs. If these postures are mastered well, they can prevent fatigue without sacrificing the beauty of demeanor.

2.坐姿(Sitting Posture)

要做到坐姿文雅并非易事,不正确的坐姿不仅不美观,还可能导致身体畸形。基本要领如下:上半身自然坐正,双腿自然弯曲,双脚平稳着地,双膝应当并拢。男士双膝可稍做分开,但女士的双膝和脚跟必须紧密靠拢。双手可半握拳置于膝盖上,或者将小臂平放在座椅两侧的扶手上,需注意从肩部到手臂要紧贴胸部,胸部微微挺起,腰部挺直,目光平视,嘴巴微微闭合,面带微笑,展现出大方自然的姿态(如图1-8所示)。

Maintaining a graceful sitting posture is not a simple skill; sitting incorrectly not only looks unattractive but may even lead to physical deformities. The basic principles are: sit up straight naturally, keep your legs bent naturally, place your feet flat on the ground, and keep your knees together. For men, the knees can be slightly apart, while for women, both the knees and heels must be kept close together. Clench your hands into a half-fist and place them on your knees, or rest your forearms flat on the armrests of the chair. Make sure to keep the area from the shoulders to the arms closely attached to the chest, keep your chest slightly out, your waist straight, your eyes level, your mouth slightly closed, and wear a smile, presenting a generous and natural demeanor (Figure 1-8).

(a) 男士坐姿　　　　　　(b) 女士坐姿　　　　　　(c) 侧面坐姿
Male Sitting Posture　　　Female Sitting Posture　　Lateral Sitting Posture

图 1-8　坐姿
Figure 1-8　Sitting Posture

依照国际惯例,坐姿包含端坐、侧坐、跪坐、盘坐等类型,由于不同国家的生活模式和风俗习惯各异,对各类坐姿也有着不同要求。在国际上,被广泛认可且最为常见的坐姿是端坐与侧坐。倘若长时间保持端坐姿势,人容易感到疲惫,此时可转换为侧坐。侧坐分为左侧坐和右侧坐两种,在遵循坐姿基本要领的前提下,身体向左(右)旋转45°,同时两脚、两膝相互靠拢。无论采用哪种坐姿,都应展现出娴雅自如的姿态,以此表达对他人的尊重,给人留下美好的印象。

According to international customs, sitting postures can be divided into formal sitting, side sitting, kneeling sitting, cross-legged sitting, etc., each with its own requirements based on different national lifestyles and customs. The most universally recognized sitting postures are formal sitting and side sitting. Sitting formally for too long can make one feel tired; at such a time, one may switch to side sitting. Side sitting can be classified into sitting sideways to the left and sitting sideways to the right. Based on the basic principles of sitting posture, turn the body 45° to the left (right), keeping the feet and knees close together. Regardless of the sitting posture, one should maintain a graceful and natural posture to show respect for others and leave a favorable impression.

3. 走姿(Walking Posture)

起步时,上身略微向前倾,将身体重心置于前脚掌上。行走过程中,应目光平视前方,保持上半身正直,做到挺胸、收腹、立腰,重心稍向前偏移,双肩平稳,双臂以肩关节为轴,自然地前后摆动。女子行走时,步伐要如同微风般轻盈。两脚行走的路线应是正对前方的一条直线,而非两条平行线,即通常所说的"猫步"。这是因为若行走时踩两条平行线,臀部便无法自然摆动,腰部也会显得僵硬,从而失去步态的优美。男子行走时,两脚跟交替向前,行进在一条直线上(但双脚形成两条平行线),两脚尖微微向外展开。

When starting to walk, lean the upper body slightly forward and shift the body's center of gravity to the front part of the foot. When walking, look ahead, keep the upper body straight, chest out, belly in, waist upright, with the center of gravity slightly forward, shoulders level, arms swinging naturally back and forth around the shoulder joints. Women should walk with a gentle and graceful gait, like a gentle breeze. The path of both feet should be straight ahead, not two parallel lines, which is commonly referred to as "catwalk". Because walking on two parallel lines would eliminate the sway of the hips and make the waist appear stiff, losing the gracefulness of the walking posture. Men walk with the heels of both feet alternately moving forward along one line while the feet form two lines, with the toes of both feet slightly turned out.

走路时,绝不能弯腰驼背,也不可以大摇大摆或者左右晃动。诸如脚尖呈外八字或内八字、脚在地面上拖着走等不良习惯,都必须加以纠正。同时,走路的时候也不能将双手插在裤兜里。此外,前厅服务人员在行走过程中,还需留意以下这些问题。

Don't hunch over, swagger or sway from side to side while walking. Bad habits such as walking with toes turned outward (in a splay-footed manner) or inward (in a pigeon-toed manner), and dragging your feet on the ground should all be corrected. Also, don't put your hands in your pockets when walking. In addition, guest service staff should pay attention to the following matters during the process of walking.

(1)在走廊、通道或楼梯上行走时,应靠右侧通行,见到宾客需主动打招呼问好。

When walking in corridors, passages or on stairs, you should keep to the right side and greet guests actively.

（2）两人一起行走时，不要手拉手或勾肩搭背；多人同行时，不要横向排成一行；与宾客一同进出时，要以礼相让，让宾客先行。

When two people are walking together, don't hold hands or put your arms around each other's shoulders. When multiple people are walking together, don't line up horizontally. When entering or exiting a place with guests, be courteous and let the guests go first.

（3）当通道较为狭窄，有宾客从对面走来时，服务员应主动停下手中的工作，侧身站立，并用手势示意，邀请宾客先行通过。

When the passage is rather narrow and there are guests coming from the opposite direction, the service staff should take the initiative to stop their work, stand sideways, and gesture with their hands to invite the guests to pass first.

（4）若有急事在身或手提重物，需要超过前方正在行走的宾客时，应先向宾客致歉，在得到宾客的许可后再超前行走，并且注意从宾客的一侧通过。若有两位宾客并排行走，切不可从他们中间穿过。

If you are in a hurry or carrying heavy items and need to overtake the guests walking in front, you should first apologize to the guests. Only after getting their permission can you move ahead, and make sure to pass by the guests from one side. If there are two guests walking side by side, never walk through the space between them.

（5）遇到极为紧急的事情时，可以加快行走步伐，但切勿惊慌失措地奔跑。

When encountering extremely urgent matters, you can quicken your pace, but never run in a flustered manner.

（6）行走过程中，严禁吸烟、吃东西、吹口哨以及整理衣物等行为。

During the process of walking, smoking, eating, whistling, and adjusting clothes are strictly prohibited.

4. 蹲姿（Squatting Posture）

许多来自欧美国家的人觉得"蹲"这一动作不够雅观，因此，他们仅在极为必要的情况下才会蹲下进行某项操作。在前厅服务工作中，当服务人员蹲下捡拾物品或系鞋带时，务必留意自身姿态，力求动作既迅速，又能展现出美观与大方的特质，始终保持大方、端庄的蹲姿。而优雅的蹲姿，通常可通过以下两种方式来实现。

Many people from Western countries consider the act of squatting inelegant, so they only squat when it is absolutely necessary. In guest service, when squatting to pick something up or tie shoelaces, pay attention to your posture. Try to be quick, aesthetically pleasing, and graceful, maintaining a dignified and proper squatting posture. Graceful squatting postures generally adopt the following two methods.

（1）交叉式蹲姿

Cross-legged Squatting Posture

下蹲时，应右脚在前，左脚在后，右小腿垂直于地面，使右脚全脚掌着地。左腿在后与右腿交叉重叠，左膝从后方伸向右侧，左脚脚跟抬起，仅脚掌着地。两腿前后紧密相靠，共同用力支撑身体。同时，臀部下沉，上身略微前倾。

When squatting, place the right foot in front and the left foot behind, with the right calf perpendicular to the ground and the entire sole of the right foot touching the floor. The left leg is positioned behind and overlaps with the right leg. The left knee reaches towards the right side from the rear, with the left heel lifted and the sole of the left foot on the ground. Both legs are closely positioned, one in front of the other, working together to support the body. The buttocks move downwards, and the upper body leans slightly forward.

（2）高低式蹲姿

High-low Squatting Posture

下蹲时，应左脚在前，右脚稍往后（两脚不重叠），两腿紧贴着向下蹲。左脚全脚掌着地，小腿大致垂直于地面，右脚脚跟抬起，脚掌着地。右膝低于左膝，左膝内侧贴靠在左小腿内侧，形成左膝高右膝低的姿势，臀部下沉，身体基本上由右腿来支撑。男性员工采用这种蹲姿时，两腿之间可保持适当的间距。而女性员工则需将两腿并拢，当穿着旗袍或短裙时更要格外注意，避免出现尴尬的情况。具体姿势如图1-9所示。

When squatting, place the left foot in front and the right foot slightly behind (not overlapping), keep both legs close together and squat downwards. The left foot is fully on the ground, and the calf is almost perpendicular to the ground, with the right heel lifted and the sole on the ground. The right knee is lower than the left knee, and the inner side of the left knee is against the inner side of the left calf, forming a posture with the left knee higher than the right knee. The body is mainly supported by the right leg as the buttocks move downwards. When male employees use this squatting posture, there can be an appropriate distance between the legs. Female employees should keep their legs close together, and they should pay more attention when wearing a cheongsam or short skirt to avoid embarrassment. As shown in Figure 1-9.

图1-9　高低式蹲姿

Figure 1-9　High-low Squatting Posture

仪容仪表对于一名服务员而言，犹如其自身的"硬件设施"，是自身固有的条件，更是成为一名服务员的先决要素，在一定程度上难以改变。不过，我们能够凭借洒脱的风度、迷人的气质以及优雅的举止等内在特质加以补充完善。优美的风度与举止，本质上是人的高尚情操、渊博学识、敏锐思辨能力等内在心理状态的自然外显。因此，前厅部员工应当致力于提升自身品格、知识储备、能力素养等诸多内在要素，进而让自己的仪容仪表呈现出一种内外协调统一的和谐美感。简而言之,就是要做到动作舒缓且轻盈,态度温和又大方,举止端庄而稳重,表情热情但含蓄。

Appearance and grooming for a server are like their personal "hardware". They are inherent qualities and essential prerequisites that are, to some extent, difficult to alter. However, we can make up for this through an easy-going demeanor, charming temperament, elegant manners, and other internal traits. Graceful demeanor and manners essentially manifest as a natural outpouring of a person's noble sentiments, profound knowledge, acute critical thinking abilities, and other internal psychological states. Therefore, guest service staff should strive to enhance their own character, knowledge reserves, and capabilities, among other internal elements, so as to make their appearance and grooming display a harmonious beauty of internal-external coordination. In short, they should ensure that their movements are gentle and light, their attitudes are amiable and generous, their manners are dignified and steady, and their expressions are warm yet reserved.

三、能适应海上的生活

Adaptability to Life at Sea

作为邮轮服务人员,大部分时间都要在海上度过。海上的生活与陆地上的生活大不相同:第一,船员的合同期通常在4至8个月之间,在此期间,他们会一直随邮轮在海上航行,无法离开邮轮,也不能回家与家人团聚;第二,由于长期在封闭环境中工作,他们的活动空间仅局限于整艘邮轮;第三,邮轮上的船员来自世界各个不同的国家,船员之间在宗教信仰、生活习惯、沟通方式等方面存在很大差异。倘若无法适应这样的工作环境,便会对船员的工作表现产生不良影响。

As a cruise service staff, who spends most of the time at sea, life at sea is quite different from that on land. Firstly, the contract period for crew members usually ranges from 4 to 8 months. During this period, crew members stay on the ship navigating the sea and are unable to leave the ship or return home to reunite with their families. Secondly, working long-term in a confined environment restricts the movement space to the entire ship. Thirdly, The crew members on the cruise ship come from various countries around the world, resulting in significant differences in religious beliefs, living habits, and communication styles among them. If crew members can't adapt to such a work environment, it will have a negative impact on their work performance.

阅读资料3(Material 3):

海上生活剪影
Snapshots of Life at Sea

倘若你看过电影《爱之船》,想必你会觉得邮轮上船员的工作堪称世界上最棒的工作之一。在邮轮上,有各种各样的欢声笑语、尽情狂欢的场景,还有浪漫迷人的海上景致,而且船员们还能搭乘奢华的邮轮环游世界。不过,邮轮上工作人员的真实生活究竟是什么样的呢?著名旅游网站"Thrillist"的报道为大家揭开了邮轮上船员们真实生活的面纱,让我们先来一探究竟吧!

If you have seen the movie "The Love Boat", you must think that working on a cruise ship is one of the best jobs in the world, with all the laughter, partying, and romantic seascapes, and the opportunity to travel the world on a luxurious liner. However, what is the real life of the crew members on board? A report by the renowned travel website "Thrillist" reveals the true lives of the crew on cruise ships, so let's take a sneak peek!

1. 员工专区(Crew Area)

尽管船员们所居住的舱室位于甲板下方,空间较为狭小,但他们却拥有一处宽敞且豪华的员工专属区域。该区域配备了运动甲板、热水浴池、运动场、酒吧以及餐厅等设施。船员们往往更多的是在这个区域里尽情享受生活。

Although crew members reside in small cabins below the deck, they possess a spacious and luxurious crew-exclusive area equipped with a sports deck, hot spring baths, sports courts, bars, and restaurants where they can fully enjoy their life.

2. 狂欢派对(Wild Party)

大家不妨想象一下电影《泰坦尼克号》里的场景。在邮轮上工作和生活,某种程度上类似于大学时期的学习生活状态,既要努力工作,又要尽情寻乐。每当夜深人静,宾客们都进入梦乡之后,船员们便开启了他们狂欢喧闹、充满激情的派对时光。

Imagine the scenes in the movie "Titanic". Life on a cruise ship is somewhat similar to college life, balancing work and fun. In the dead of night, when guests are fast asleep, the crew kick off their own wild parties.

3. 没有休假(No Days Off)

根据合同规定,在连续4至10个月的时间里,船员每周都需工作7天。这表明船员根本没有休息日,所以只能在工作的间隙抽空放松一下。

According to the contract, crew members must work 7 days a week for 4 to 10 consecutive months. This means crew members have no days off at all, and relaxation can only be squeezed into short intervals between work duties.

4. 工作时间(Working Hours)

在船上工作有时会让人感到无比抓狂,这是因为船员肩负着相应的职责,必须随时待命,做到随叫随到。有时,船员们甚至可能连续工作15周,且每周的工作时长超过100小时。

Work on board can be extremely frustrating as crew members are required to be on call at all times. There are times when crew members work 15 weeks straight, accumulating more than 100 hours weekly.

5. 容易存钱(Easy Savings)

在邮轮上,部分岗位能收获颇为丰厚的小费,并且其薪资水平与陆地上的诸多工作不相上下。与此同时,船员们无须承担食宿费用,也不必为日常通勤而烦恼。这意味着在船上的生活几乎没有额外开销,如此一来,船员们便能轻松积攒下一笔可观的财富。

Some positions on cruise ships receive quite substantial tips, and the salaries for these positions are comparable to those of other jobs on land. Since crew members don't have to pay for accommodation fees or transportation costs, their living expenses are virtually nil, enabling them to easily amass a considerable sum of money.

6. 单独供餐(Separate Meals)

许多人都认为船员们与宾客们享用的食物是相同的,可事实并非如此。船员们有专属的独立餐厅,然而那里烹饪出来的菜肴并不怎么令人垂涎。

Contrary to popular belief, crew members don't partake in the same cuisine as guests. They have their own dining hall, though the culinary offerings may not be particularly appealing.

7. 国籍众多(Diverse Nationalities)

在邮轮上工作,能够接触到来自世界各国的宾客。事实上,有些邮轮上的船员甚至来自 60 多个不同的国家,所以在船上了解不同国家的文化习俗,是一件非常有意思的事情。

Working on a cruise ship exposes you to guests from around the globe, and crew members on some cruise ships even come from over 60 different countries. Learning about various cultures and customs on board is quite an interesting experience.

8. 等级分明(Strictly Hierarchical)

邮轮上有着清晰明确的等级制度,船上员工分为三类,分别是高级职员、工作人员(例如舞者、演奏师、荷官以及礼品店收银员等)和普通员工(例如调酒师、服务员和客舱服务员等)。不同类别的人员享受不同待遇,举例来说,高级职员能够与宾客一同观看表演,还能上岸参观港口;然而,其他船员则不被允许随意离船上岸,并且在非值班期间,也不允许随意进出非员工区域。

The cruise ship environment is strictly hierarchical, with three distinct categories: Officers, Staff (such as dancers, musicians, casino dealers, and gift shop cashiers), and Crew (such as bartenders, waiters, and cabin attendants). Each category enjoys different privileges; for example, Officers may watch performances with guests and go ashore to visit ports, whereas other crew members are not free to leave the ship or enter non-crew areas during their off-duty hours.

9. 高效工作(High Efficiency)

船员们具备超高的工作效率。在陆地上,没有任何一家餐厅能与邮轮餐厅相媲美。邮轮上的餐厅能在 15 分钟内可容纳 900 人等待就餐。通常每艘邮轮设有 2 处餐厅,每处餐厅有 2 个就餐时间段,这就意味着船员们要在 5 个小时内,为 3500 名宾客提供就餐服务。

The crew members demonstrate exceptionally high work efficiency. No restaurant on land can rival a cruise ship's dining facility, which can seat 900 people within 15 minutes. Typically, with two restaurants and two meal sittings per restaurant on each ship, the crew must serve 3500 guests within 5 hours.

10. 迅速轮换(Swift Turnaround)

有时候,邮轮需要在 3 小时内为下一次航行做好准备。在港口停靠妥当后,需迅速安排几千名宾客下船,对整艘邮轮进行清理,完成船员的轮班调配,之后以全新的面貌等待下一批宾客登船。

Sometimes, the cruise ship needs to get ready for the next voyage within just 3 hours after docking at a port. This involves getting thousands of guests to disembark quickly, cleaning the entire ship, adjusting crew shifts, and then presenting the ship in a fresh state for the next group of visitors to come aboard.

三、具备较强的服务意识
Strong Service Orientation

邮轮旅游的独特之处,很大程度体现在其服务水平上。通常,船员与宾客的比例越高,意味着服务水平越高。此外,邮轮服务人员还需热情周到、亲切真诚,对待每一位宾客都一视同仁,要有主动为宾客提供优质服务的意识,这是提升邮轮服务质量的关键所在。强烈的服务意识,既是邮轮服务人员从业的前提条件,也是其最基本的职业素养之一。微笑服务,作为服务意识的主要体现方式之一,也是邮轮对服务人员的核心要求。

The uniqueness of cruising lies in its level of service; the higher the ratio of crew to guests, the higher the service standard. Cruise service staff must be enthusiastic, considerate, sincere and treat every guest equally, taking the initiative to provide excellent service to guests, which is key to improving cruise service quality. A strong sense of service is a prerequisite for cruise service staff employment and a fundamental professional quality. Smiling service is one of the principal expressions of service awareness and a key requirement for cruise service staff.

四、具备较高的英语水平
High Level of English Proficiency

邮轮工作具有高度的国际化特征,服务对象来自世界各地,服务人员也来自不同国家,工作空间更是跨越国界。所以,具备较强的语言应用能力是邮轮员工的基本素质。当下,英语是各大国际豪华邮轮上通用的工作语言。而且,语言应用能力越强,在邮轮上获得重用的机会就越多,晋升的可能性越大,在同类岗位上所享受的待遇也会越高。

Working on a cruise ship is a highly international affair, serving an international clientele by an international crew in an international working environment. Therefore, strong language skills are a basic qualification for cruise ship employees. At present, English is the working language on major international luxury cruise ships. The better your command of the language, the greater your chances of promotion and higher pay for the same position.

由于邮轮前厅部员工的工作性质,他们的英语水平相较于其他部门员工需要更高。前厅部员工需能够流利地运用英语与宾客进行对话沟通,妥善处理各类英文材料,并且熟练操作前台管理系统。

Cruise guest service staff, in particular, need to have an even higher level of English compared to staff in other departments, who are capable of conversing fluently with guests, handling various English documents, and operating the front desk management system proficiently.

五、具备较高的沟通能力
Advanced Communication Skills

邮轮服务人员需妥善处理与宾客、同事以及上下级之间的关系。在邮轮上,服务人员和宾客均来自不同国家,人际交往过程中,既存在文化冲突,又涉及利益关联。这便要求邮轮服务人员熟知宾客和同事所属国家的文化习俗,具备较强的沟通意识,掌握人际沟通的原则,拥有出色的沟通交流技能与能力,并积极主动地开展交流。

Cruise service staff must handle relationships with guests, colleagues, and superiors effectively. On cruise ships, both service staff and guests come from diverse countries. Navigating cultural differences and aligning interests requires cruise service staff to understand the cultural norms and customs of their guests and colleagues, possess a strong awareness of communication, grasp interpersonal communication principles, and have excellent communication skills to interact actively.

除了上述几点,作为一名优秀的前厅部员工,还应具备稳定的心理素质、认真负责的工作态度、娴熟的专业技能、丰富的专业知识以及广泛的知识面等素养。

Beyond these aspects, an outstanding guest service staff should also have a stable psychological state, a conscientious work attitude, proficient professional skills, rich professional knowledge, and a broad range of knowledge.

实训任务考核指南
Training Task Assessment Guide

实训任务 Training Task	分值(分) Score (Points)	实际得分 Actual Score
仪容仪表、礼貌礼节 Grooming, Politeness and Etiquette	20	
站姿 Standing Posture	20	
坐姿 Sitting Posture	20	
走姿 Walking Posture	20	
蹲姿 Squatting Time	20	
【合计】 Total	100	

模块 2

登离船服务

Module 2

Boarding and Disembarkation Service

登船准备工作　项目 1
Preparation for Boarding　Project 1

任务 1　登船手续所需信息
Mission 1
Information Required for Boarding Procedures

实训目的
Training Objectives

　　教师示范讲解登船宾客信息资料的处理程序,随后学生针对宾客登船信息资料展开分析整理训练。借此,学生能够了解并掌握如何针对不同宾客,做好相应的登船服务准备工作,进而达到熟知操作程序与操作规范的训练要求。

Through the teacher's demonstration and explanation of the boarding guest information processing procedures, enabling students to analyze and organize the guest boarding information, so that students can understand and master how to prepare for the corresponding boarding service for different guests, and meet the training requirements of familiarizing themselves with operation procedures and operation specifications.

实训方法
Training Method

　　首先,教师进行示范讲解。随后,将学生分成每组 6 人的小组,依据宾客登船资料分析处理时与相关岗位沟通的需求进行配置,设置登船部登船专员、酒店部专员、会员部专员、客舱部专员、岸上部门专员、管家部专员等岗位。各小组成员分别扮演对应岗位员工以及宾客，模拟在登船资料分析与处理过程中与邮轮各部门沟通的场景。在学生模拟训练期间，教师加以指导，学生通过反复强化训练，以实现熟练掌握该项操作技能的目标。

First, the teacher will conduct a demonstration and give an explanation. Then, the students will be divided into groups of six. Based on the communication requirements with relevant positions during the analysis and processing of guest boarding data, positions such as boarding specialists in the boarding department specialists, hotel department specialists, membership department specialists, cabin department specialists, shore-side department specialists, and housekeeping department specialists will be set up. Each group member will play the roles of employees in corresponding positions and guests, simulating the scenarios of communicating with various departments of the cruise ship during the analysis and processing of boarding data. During the students' simulation training, the teacher will provide guidance, and the students will carry out repeated intensive training to achieve the goal of mastering this operational skill proficiently.

实训准备 Training Preparation

信息：宾客名单、有特殊要求的宾客名单、重要宾客名单、会员资料、宾客历史档案。

Information: the list of guests, the list of guests with special requirements, the list of important guests, membership information, guest historical records.

实训内容及操作标准 Training Content and Operating Standards

作为一名合格的邮轮登船部服务员，不仅要有扎实的登船服务理论知识，更重要的是熟练掌握宾客登船信息资料。一般而言，除了核验重要物品与证件、引导宾客登船，邮轮登船部服务员的专业技能主要体现在对宾客登船信息资料的分析与处理上，具体程序如下：

As a qualified cruise boarding department staff, in addition to having solid theoretical knowledge of boarding services, it is crucial to master guest boarding information proficiently. Usually, in addition to verifying important items and documents and guiding guests to board the ship, the skills of cruise boarding department staff are mainly demonstrated through the analysis and processing of guests' boarding information. The specific procedures are as follows：

宾客登船资料分析处理的程序（Procedures for the Analysis and Processing of Guest Boarding Data）：

1.宾客在登船前，可从岸上部门获取本航次的相关宾客信息，其中包括宾客名单、有特殊要求的宾客名单、重要宾客名单、会员资料以及宾客历史档案。

Before boarding the ship, guests can obtain relevant information about guests of this voyage from the shore department. This information includes the guest list, the list of guests with special requirements, the list of important guests, membership information, and guest historical records.

2.分析处理有特殊要求的宾客名单,针对有特殊需求的宾客,提前通知相关部门,做好提供个性化服务的准备。例如:若有穆斯林宾客,登船部服务员应在第一时间通知餐饮部,以便其做好菜品调整。

Analyze and process the list of guests with special requirements. For those guests with special needs, notify the relevant departments in advance to prepare to provide personalized services. For example, if there are Muslim guests, the staff of the boarding department should inform the catering department immediately to adjust the dishes.

3.分析处理重要宾客名单。针对贵宾,提前筹备特别服务与相应礼节,例如提供个性化迎宾服务、优先登船服务,确保其在收费餐厅和娱乐活动方面拥有优先预订权,安排海上管家全程热线服务及专属服务柜台等,并提前通知相关部门做好贵宾接待服务。

Analyze and process the list of important guests. For VIP guests, make advance preparations for special services and corresponding courtesies. For instance, offer personalized welcome services, priority boarding services, ensure their priority reservation rights for paid restaurants and entertainment activities, arrange for the sea butler's full-course hotline service and an exclusive service counter, etc. Also, notify the relevant departments in advance to prepare for VIP reception services.

4.分析处理会员资料。提前收集会员信息,依据相关标准对会员进行等级划分,针对不同级别的会员,筹备与之对应的会员礼遇。

Analyze and process the membership information. Collect membership information in advance and classify members according to relevant criteria. For members at different levels, make preparations for the corresponding membership privileges.

5.分析宾客历史档案。借助电脑查询登船宾客的乘船偏好、过往在邮轮上的消费习惯等相关信息,依据不同宾客的历史档案,做好提供个性化服务的准备。

Analyze the historical records of guests. Use a computer to look up information such as the boarding preferences of guests and their previous consumption habits on cruise ships. Based on the guest history files of different guests, make preparations to provide personalized services.

宾客登船资料分析处理程序图解
Illustration of Guest Boarding Data Analysis and Processing Procedure

1. 获取航次游客的相关信息
Get Relevant Information about Tourists

2. 分析处理有特殊要求的游客名单
Analyze and Deal with the List of Tourists with Special Requirements

3. 分析处理重要游客名单
Analyze and Deal with the List of Important Tourists

模块2 登离船服务
Module 2 Boarding and Disembarkation Service

4.分析处理会员资料
Analyze and Process Member Information

5.分析游客历史档案
Analyze the Historical Archives of Tourists

实训任务考核指南
Training Task Assessment Guide

实训任务 Training Task	分值(分) Score（Points）	实际得分 Actual Score
仪容仪表、礼貌礼节 Grooming, Politeness and Etiquette	10	
宾客资料获取 Acquisition of Guest Information	20	
宾客资料分析 Analysis of Guest Information	20	
宾客服务准备 Preparation for Guest Services	40	
操作时间 Operating Time	10	
【合计】 Total	100	

项目 2　登船服务流程
Project 2　Boarding Service Process

任务 1　散客登船
Mission 1　Individual Guests Board the Ship

实训目的
Training Objectives

通过教师对散客登船程序的示范讲解以及学生围绕散客登船程序展开的训练,使学生了解并掌握散客登船流程,达成熟知操作程序与操作规范的训练要求。

Through the teacher's demonstration and explanation of the boarding procedure for individual guests, and the students' training on this procedure, the students can understand and master the boarding process of individual guests, meeting the training requirements of being familiar with the operation procedures and operation specifications.

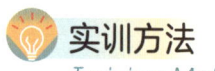
实训方法
Training Method

首先,由教师进行示范讲解。之后,将学生分成每组 6 人的小组,按照宾客登船流程进行登船部岗位配置,设置登船部经理、副经理、登船专员、证件管理专员、清关员、引导员等岗位。各小组成员分别扮演登船部员工和宾客,模拟散客宾客登船操作程序。在学生模拟训练过程中,教师予以指导,学生反复强化训练。小组模拟训练结束后进行情景展示,接着师生、生生展开研讨评价,以此达到熟练掌握该项操作技能的目的。

First of all, the teacher will conduct a demonstration and explanation. Then, the students will be grouped into teams of six. According to the guest boarding process, positions in the Boarding Department will be allocated, including the boarding department manager, deputy manager, boarding commissioner, certificate management specialist, customs clearance officer, and guide. Each team member will play the roles of both boarding department staff and guests to simulate the boarding operation procedures for individual guests. During the students' simulation training, teachers will provide guidance, and students will carry out repeated intensive training. After the group simulation training, a scenario display will be held. Subsequently, teachers and students, as well as among students, will conduct discussions and evaluations to achieve the goal of proficiently mastering this operational skill.

实训准备
Training Preparation

信息:邮轮登船系统、电脑、护照阅读器、制卡机、打印机、电话、船卡、宾客有效证件(护照或有效身份证明)、健康申报表、宾客信用卡等。

Information: cruise boarding system, computer, passport reader, ship card making machine, printer, telephone, ship card, guest valid certificate (passport or valid identification), health declaration form, guest credit card, etc.

实训内容及操作标准
Training Content and Operating Standards

作为一名合格的邮轮登船部服务员应熟练掌握登船服务流程,能熟练地为散客办理登船手续。具体程序如下:

As a qualified cruise boarding department attendant, you should be proficient in the boarding service process and be proficient in handling the boarding procedures for individual guests. The specific procedures are as follows:

散客宾客登船程序(Boarding Procedures for Individual Guests):

1.抵达邮轮码头(Arrive at the Cruise Terminal)

宾客在指定时段抵达邮轮码头,登船部引导员负责欢迎并为宾客提供问询服务。

Guests arrive at the cruise terminal during the designated time period, and the boarding department guide is responsible for welcoming them and providing inquiry services.

2.托运行李(Checked Luggage)

宾客到达行李托运处办理行李托运,行李托运处工作人员应指导宾客填写邮轮专用的行李牌并系到行李上,交由行李员运至客舱门口;提醒宾客携带的小件行李可自行提上船,无须托运;建议宾客将重要证件及贵重物品自行携带上船。

When guests arrive at the luggage check-in area, the staff there should guide the guests to fill out the cruise-specific luggage tags and attach them to the luggage, and then hand the luggage over to the porters to be transported to the cabin door. They should remind guests that small carry-on luggage can be taken on board without check-in, and suggest that guests carry important documents and valuables with them on board.

3. 办理登记并关联信用卡(Register and Associate a Credit Card)

(1)向宾客问好,询问是否需要办理登记;

Greet the guests and ask if they need to go through the check-in procedures;

(2)请宾客出示登船通行证、护照、签证、家庭法律文件等登船文件并核对信息;

Ask the guests to present their boarding passes, passports, visas, family legal documents and other boarding documents, and then check the information;

(3)采集护照信息;

Collect the passport information;

(4)在邮轮登船系统中办理登记;

Complete the check-in process in the cruise boarding system;

(5)打印邮轮登船卡;

Print the cruise boarding card;

(6)询问宾客是否需要将信用卡与邮轮船卡绑定,并开通船卡的消费功能;

Ask the guests if they want to bind their credit cards to the cruise ship cards and activate the consumption function of the ship cards;

(7)请宾客出示国际信用卡;

Ask the guests to show their international credit cards;

(8)注册信用卡,取得宾客信用卡的预授权,并请宾客在预授权单上签字;

Register the credit card, obtain the pre-authorization of the guest's credit card, and ask the guest to sign the pre-authorization form;

(9)将信用卡、邮轮船卡、护照、签证、家庭法律文件等交还给宾客;

Return the credit cards, cruise ship cards, passports, visas, family legal documents, etc. to the guests;

(10)向宾客道别。

Say goodbye to the guests.

4. 安全检查(Security Inspection)

根据安全检查要求,对宾客进行身体和所携带物品及行李的检查。

According to the requirements of the security inspection, conduct inspections on the guests' bodies, the items they carry and their luggage.

5. 办理"一关两检"(Apply for "One Custom and Two Inspections")

"一关"是指海关检查,"两检"是指检验检疫和边防检查。

The "one custom" refers to the customs inspection, and the "two inspections" refer to the inspection and quarantine and the border inspection.

6.护照收集(Passport Collection)

将宾客的护照统一收集保管,在各停靠港停靠之前办理出入境手续。

Unify to collect and keep guests' passports, and go through the entry and exit procedures before stopping at each port of call.

7.相片采集(Photo Collection)

查验各个宾客的邮轮船卡,要求宾客进行登船安检拍照,照片信息存入邮轮系统中并与邮轮船卡关联,用于宾客上下船面部扫描对比。

Check the cruise ship cards of each guest and ask the guests to go through the boarding security check and have their photos taken. The photo information is stored in the cruise system and associated with the cruise ship cards, which is used for face-scanning and comparison when guests board and disembark the ship.

8.廊桥登船(Boarding on the Covered Bridge)

指引宾客登船并找到自己的舱房。

Guide guests to board the ship and find their own cabins.

散客登船程序图解
Illustration of the Boarding Procedure for Individual Guests

1.抵达邮轮码头
Arrive at the Cruise Terminal

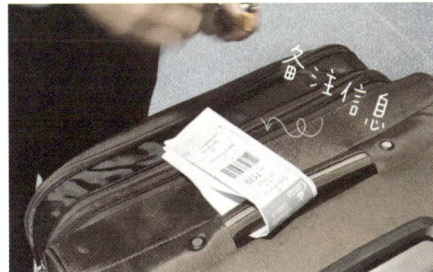

2.托运行李
Checked Luggage

3.办理登记并关联信用卡
Register and Associate Credit Cards

4.安全检查
Security Inspection

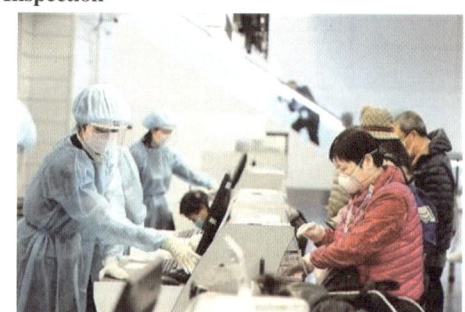

5.办理"一关两检"
Apply for "One Custom and Two Inspections"

6.护照收集
Passport Collection

模块2　登离船服务
Module 2　Boarding and Disembarkation Service

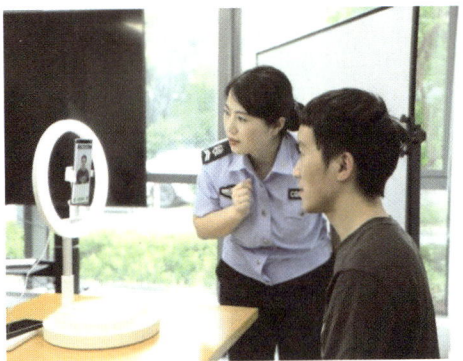

7.相片采集
Photo Collection

8.登船
Boarding

实训任务考核指南
Training Task Assessment Guide

实训任务 Training Task	分值(分) Score（Points）	实际得分 Actual Score
仪容仪表、礼貌礼节 Grooming，Politeness and Etiquette	10	
操作程序 Operating Procedure	20	
操作质量 Operating Quality	20	
操作熟练度 Operating Proficiency	40	
操作时间 Operating Time	10	
【合计】 Total	100	

任务 2　团队宾客登船
Mission 2
Group Guests Board the Ship

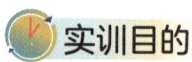

实训目的
Training Objectives

通过教师对团队宾客登船程序的示范讲解，学生对团队宾客登船程序的训练，使学生了解和掌握团队宾客登船流程，达到熟知操作程序与操作规范的训练要求。

Through the teacher's demonstration and explanation of the boarding procedures for group guests and the students' training on these procedures, students can understand and master the boarding process of group guests, thus meeting the training requirements of being familiar with the operation procedures and norms.

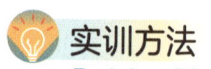

实训方法
Training Method

首先由教师进行示范讲解，然后学生分成每组4人的小组，将所有小组分为宾客组、登船部、行李托运处、护照收集组、相片采集处、安检处、旅行社领队组，按照宾客登船流程进行岗位分配。各小组组员按分配到的岗位进行岗位工作模拟，分别扮演不同的身份，模拟团队宾客登船操作程序。在学生模拟训练过程中，教师进行指导，学生反复强化训练，小组模拟训练后进行情景展示，师生、生生研讨评价，达到熟练掌握该项操作技能的目的。

First, the teacher will demonstrate and explain. Then, the students will be divided into groups of four. All the groups will be divided into the guest group, boarding department, luggage check-in area, passport collection group, photo-taking area, security inspection area, and travel agency team-leader group, and job assignments will be made according to the guest boarding process. Each group member conducts job-related simulations according to the assigned position, takes on different roles, and simulates the operation procedures for group guests to board the ship. During the students' simulation training, teachers provide guidance. The students conduct repeated intensive training. After the group simulation training, there will be a scenario presentation. Teachers and students, as well as students among themselves, will conduct discussions and evaluations to achieve the goal of mastering this operational skill proficiently.

实训准备 Training Preparation

信息：领队旗、邮轮登船系统、电脑、护照阅读器、制卡机、打印机、电话、船卡、宾客有效证件（护照或有效身份证明）、健康申报表、宾客信用卡等。

Information: leader flag, cruise boarding system, computer, passport reader, card-making machine, printer, telephone, ship card, guest valid certificate (passport or valid identification), health declaration form, guest credit card, etc.

实训内容及操作标准 Training Content and Operating Standards

作为一名合格的邮轮登船部服务员应熟练掌握登船服务流程，能熟练地为团队宾客办理登船手续。具体程序如下：

As a qualified attendant in the cruise boarding department, one should be proficient in the boarding service and be proficient in handling the boarding procedures for group guests. The specific procedures are as follows:

团队宾客登船程序（Boarding Procedures for Group Guests）：

1. 码头集合（Gather at the Dock）

宾客在指定时段抵达邮轮码头，登船部引导员负责欢迎并为宾客提供问询服务，引导宾客领取船票（或护照、签证、家庭法律文件等）。

When guests arrive at the cruise terminal at the designated time, the boarding department guide is responsible for welcoming and providing inquiry services for guests, and guiding guests to collect tickets (or passports, visas, family legal documents, etc.).

2. 托运行李（Checked Luggage）

宾客到达行李托运处办理行李托运，行李托运处工作人员应指导宾客填写邮轮专用的行李牌并系到行李上，交由行李员运至客舱门口；提醒宾客携带的小件行李可自行提上船，无须托运；建议宾客将重要证件及贵重物品自行携带上船。

When guests arrive at the luggage check-in area, the staff there should guide the guests to fill out the cruise-specific luggage tags and attach them to their luggage, and then hand the luggage over to the porters to be transported to the cabin doors. They should remind guests that small items of luggage they carry can be taken on board without checking. Also, it is advisable to suggest that guests carry important documents and valuables with them when boarding the ship.

3.柜台登记（前五部分可由旅行社领队代为办理）Counter Registration（the First Five Parts Can Be Handled by the Travel Agency Leader）

（1）向宾客问好，询问是否需要办理登记；
Say hello to the guests and ask if they need to register；
（2）请宾客出示登船通行证、护照、签证、家庭法律文件等登船文件并核对信息；
Please ask the guests to show their boarding passes, passports, visas, family legal documents and other boarding documents and then check the information；
（3）采集护照信息；
Collect passport information；
（4）在邮轮登船系统中办理登记；
Register in the cruise boarding system；
（5）打印邮轮登船卡；
Print the cruise boarding card；
（6）询问宾客是否需要将信用卡与邮轮船卡绑定，并开通船卡的消费功能；
Ask guests if they need to bind the credit card to the cruise ship card and open the consumption function of the ship card；
（7）请宾客出示国际信用卡；
Please ask the guests to show their international credit cards；
（8）注册信用卡，取得宾客信用卡的预授权，并请宾客在预授权单上签字；
Register a credit card, obtain the pre-authorization of the guest's credit card, and ask the guest to sign the pre-authorization form；
（9）将信用卡、邮轮船卡、护照、签证、家庭法律文件等交还给宾客；
Return credit cards, cruise ship cards, passports, visas, family legal documents, etc. to guests；
（10）向宾客道别。
Say goodbye to guests.

4.安全检查（Security Inspection）

根据安全检查要求，对宾客进行身体和所携带物品及行李的检查。
According to the requirements of the security inspection, conduct inspections on the guests' bodies, the items they carry and their luggage.

5.办理"一关两检"（Apply for "One Custom and Two Inspections"）

"一关"是指海关检查，"两检"是指检验检疫和边防检查。
The "one custom" refers to the customs inspection, and the "two inspections" refer to the inspection and quarantine and the border inspection.

6.护照收集（Passport Collection）

将宾客的护照统一收集保管，在各停靠港停靠之前办理出入境手续。

Unify to collect and keep guests' passports, and go through the entry and exit procedures before stopping at each port of call.

7. 相片采集(Photo Collection)

查验各个宾客的邮轮船卡,要求宾客进行登船安检拍照,照片信息存入邮轮系统中并与邮轮船卡关联,用于宾客上下船面部扫描对比。

Check the cruise ship cards of each guest, and ask the guests to go through the boarding security check and have their photos taken. The photo information is stored in the cruise system and associated with the cruise ship cards, which is used for face scanning and comparison when guests board and disembark the ship.

8. 廊桥登船(Boarding on the Covered Bridge)

指引宾客登船并找到自己的舱房。

Guide guests to board the ship and find their own cabins.

团队宾客登船程序图解
Illustration of the Boarding Procedure for Group Guests

1. 码头集合
Gather at the Dock

2. 托运行李
Check Luggage

3.办理登记并关联信用卡
Register and Associate Credit Cards

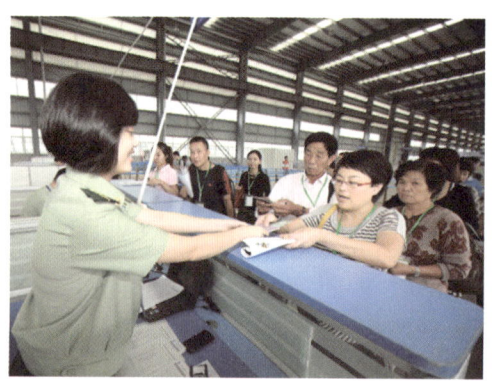
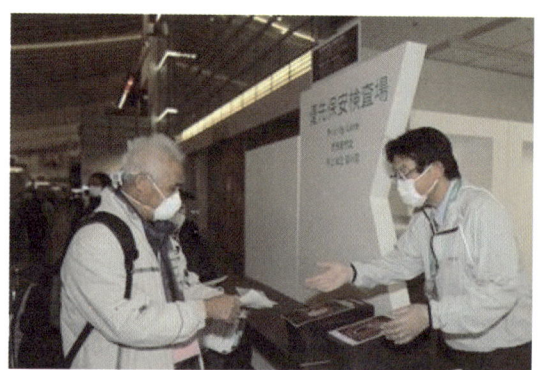

4.安全检查
Security Inspection

5 办理"一关两检"
Apply for "One Custom and Two Inspections"

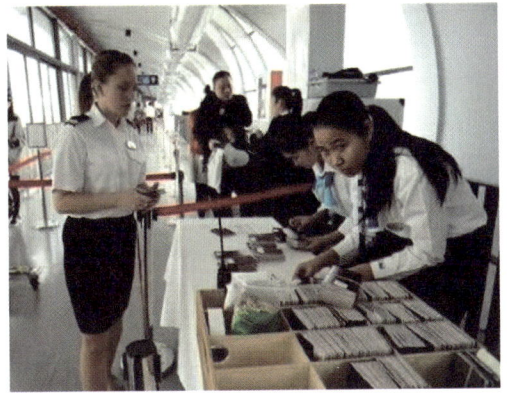
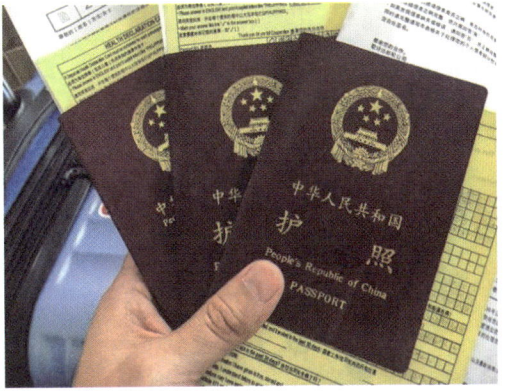

6.护照收集
Passport Collection

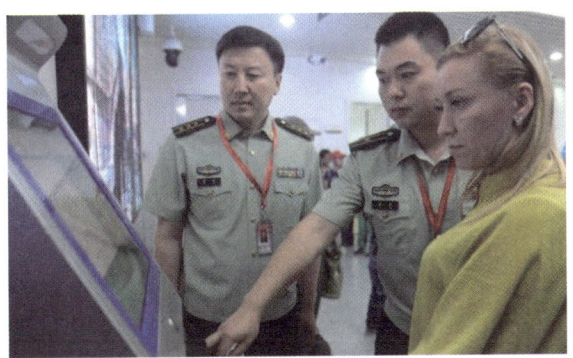

7.相片采集
Photo Collection

8.登船
Boarding

实训任务考核指南
Training Task Assessment Guide

实训任务 Training Task	分值(分) Score（Points）	实际得分 Actual Score
仪容仪表、礼貌礼节 Grooming, Politeness and Etiquette	10	
操作程序 Operating Procedure	20	
操作质量 Operating Quality	20	
操作熟练度 Operating Proficiency	40	
操作时间 Operating Time	10	
【合计】 Total	100	

登船服务实例 项目 3
Examples of Boarding Service / Project 3

任务 1 在线登记
Mission 1 Online Registration

实训目的
Training Objectives

教师示范讲解在线登记程序，随后学生进行在线登记程序的训练。借此，学生能够了解并掌握在线登记流程，进而达到熟知操作程序与操作规范的训练要求。

Through the teacher's demonstration and explanation of the online registration procedure, followed by the students' training on the online registration procedure, students can understand and master the online registration process and thus meet the training requirements of being familiar with the operating procedures and operating specifications.

实训方法
Training Method

首先，教师进行示范讲解，随后学生模拟宾客身份，开展在线登记操作训练。在学生模拟训练期间，教师予以指导，学生通过反复强化练习，从而达成熟练掌握该项操作技能的目标。

First, the teacher will conduct a demonstration and give an explanation. Subsequently, the students will simulate the roles of guests to carry out online registration operation training. During the students' simulation training, the teacher will offer guidance, and the students will conduct repeated intensive training to achieve the goal of mastering this operational skill proficiently.

实训准备 Training Preparation

信息：宾客名单、宾客有效证件（护照或有效身份证明）、邮轮行程前后的旅行计划表、宾客信用卡等。

Information: list of guests, valid guest documents (passport or valid identification), travel schedule before and after the cruise itinerary, guest credit card, etc.

实训内容及操作标准 Training Content and Operating Standards

作为一名合格的邮轮登船部服务员，不仅要具备扎实的登船服务理论知识，更重要的是熟练掌握在线登记程序。通常而言，除引导宾客登船外，邮轮登船部服务员还需掌握在线登记的相关程序，以便为宾客提供更优质的服务，具体程序如下：

As a qualified cruise boarding department staff, in addition to having solid theoretical knowledge of boarding service, it is more important to master online registration procedures. Usually, in addition to guiding guests to board the ship, cruise boarding department staff also need to master the relevant procedures of online registration in order to provide better services for guests. The specific procedures are as follows:

在线登记程序（Online Registration Procedure）：

一、以"爱达·魔都号"邮轮为例
Take Adora Magic City Cruise as an Example

1.登录邮轮官网，在官网页面找到并点击"在线值船"选项，随即开启在线值船操作；也可使用支付宝、微信扫描专属二维码，直接进入邮轮在线值船小程序。

Log in to the cruise ship's official website. Locate and click the "Online Check-in" option on the website page to start the online check-in process. Alternatively, scan the exclusive QR code with Alipay or WeChat to directly access the cruise ship's online check-in miniprogram.

2.请填写宾客个人资料。进入行前值船程序后，开始上传个人信息。在弹出的会员界面中点击"同意"，即可享受会员专享福利，然后完成所有操作步骤。

Please fill in the guests' personal information. After entering the pre-departure check-in procedure, start uploading personal information. Click "Agree" on the pop-up membership interface, and then you can enjoy the exclusive benefits for members and complete all the operation steps.

3.查看宾客的船票信息,内容包含个人姓名、乘坐船只、出发日期、码头房间号和订票号等,然后逐一确认信息是否存在错漏之处。

Check the guests' ship ticket information. The information includes the individual's name, the ship they will board, the departure date, the dock room number, and the ticket booking number, etc. Then, carefully verify one by one whether there are any errors or omissions in the information.

4.确认宾客已阅读登船须知。请宾客仔细研读船票下方的注意事项,同时也可了解一下船上的精彩活动。

Make sure that guests have read the boarding instructions. Please ask the guests to carefully study the precautions below the ship ticket, and at the same time, they can also learn about the wonderful activities on the ship.

5.打印上船通行证。

Print the boarding pass.

二、以皇家加勒比邮轮为例
Take the Royal Caribbean Cruise as an Example

1.登录邮轮官方网站。点击"已有预订"选项,选择"在线值船"功能。

Log in to the official website of the cruise ship. Click on the "Existing Reservation" option and select the "Online Ship Check-In" function.

2.验证资料。逐一确认信息是否存在错漏之处。若拼音姓名与护照上的拼音姓名不一致,需立即联系旅行社工作人员;若中文姓名与护照上的中文姓名不一致,可直接将其修改为与护照上一致的内容。

Verify the materials. Confirm one by one whether there are any errors or omissions in the information. If the pinyin name is inconsistent with the pinyin name on the passport, you need to contact the staff of the travel agency immediately. If the Chinese name is inconsistent with the Chinese name on the passport, you can directly modify it to be the same as that on the passport.

3.填写宾客登船信息。

Fill in the boarding information of the guests.

4.选择消费方式。

Choose the consumption method.

5.生成登船凭证并打印。

Generate the boarding pass and print it.

在线登记程序图解
Diagram of Online Registration Procedure

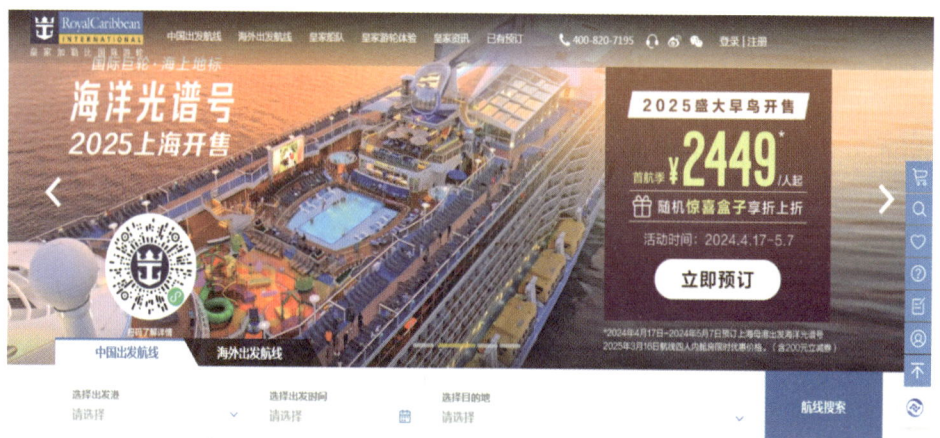

1.登录邮轮官网

Log in to the Official Website of the Cruise

2.填写登录信息

Fill in the Login Information

模块2 登离船服务
Module 2 Boarding and Disembarkation Service

出发日前72小时前可在线值船，并完整打印登船证，为保障您的信息安全性，请在15分钟内填写完毕。

| 第一步 验证资料 | 第二步 填写登船信息 | 第三步 选择消费方式 | 第四步 日本入境卡 | 第五步 生成登船证 |

带 * 号的为必填

* 姓（拼音）：
* 出生日期：
* 所乘游轮：   海洋光谱号
* 出航日期：
* ○皇家预订号 ●舱房号

☐ 我已阅读并同意《乘客票据合同（包括乘客行为守则和拒绝承运政策）》
在提交资料及后续填写相关信息前，请务必阅读和了解 《隐私政策》

3.验证资料并填写个人信息
Verify and Fill in the Personal Information

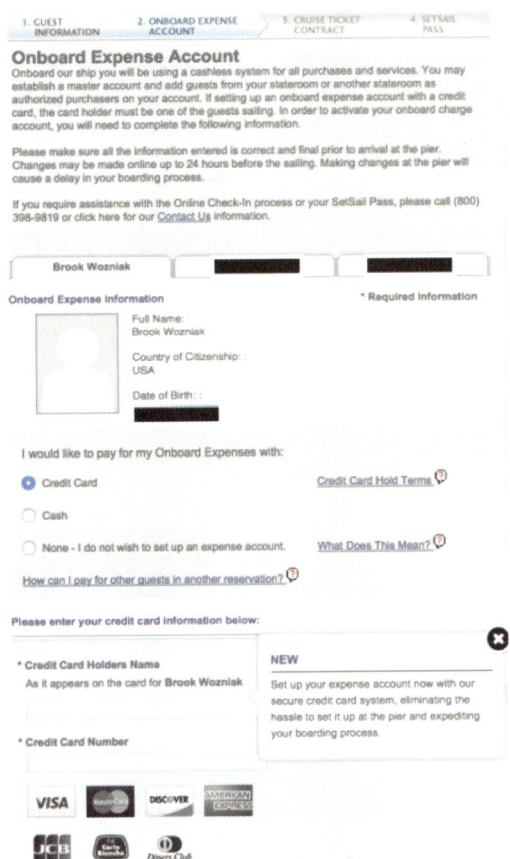

4.选择消费方式
Choose the Consumption Methods

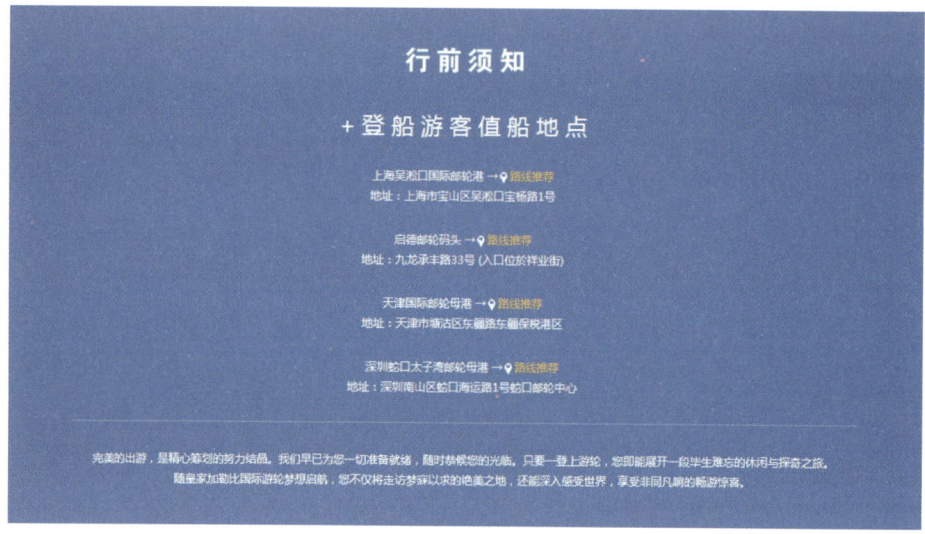

5.确认宾客阅读登船须知
Confirm that Guests Read the Boarding Instructions

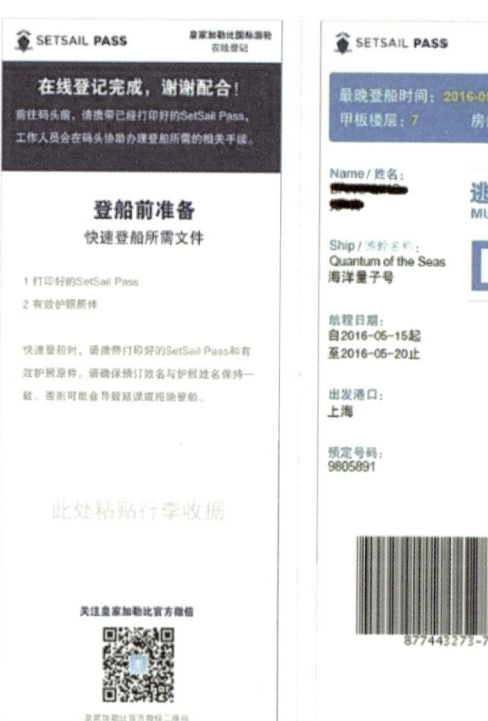

6.打印上船通行证
Print the Boarding Pass

模块2 登离船服务
Module 2 Boarding and Disembarkation Service

实训任务考核指南
Training Task Assessment Guide

实训任务 Training Task	分值(分) Score (Points)	实际得分 Actual Score
仪容仪表、礼貌礼节 Grooming, Politeness and Etiquette	10	
操作程序 Operating Procedure	20	
操作质量 Operating Quality	20	
操作熟练度 Operating Proficiency	40	
操作时间 Operating Time	10	
【合计】 Total	100	

登船常见问题处理　项目 4
Handling of Frequently Asked Questions about Boarding　Project 4

任务 1　常见问题处理
Mission 1　Handling of Frequently Asked Questions

实训目的
Training Objectives

　　通过教师对登船常见问题处理程序的示范讲解,学生对登船常见案例的分析训练,使学生了解和掌握登船常见问题的处理程序,达到熟知操作程序与操作规范的训练要求。

Through the teacher's demonstration and explanation of the procedures for handling of frequently asked questions, and students' analysis and training on common boarding cases, students can understand and master the procedures for handling common boarding problems, and meet the training requirements of familiarity with operation procedures and norms.

实训方法
Training Method

　　首先由教师进行示范讲解登船常见问题处理的一般程序,并准备一定数量的常见案例。学生分成每组 4 人的小组并选派一位小组长到教师处抽取案例。各小组组员按抽取到的案例进行分析处理模拟,分别扮演不同的身份(宾客和工作人员)。在学生模拟训练过程中,教师进行指导,学生反复强化训练,小组模拟训练后进行情景展示,师生、生生研讨评价,达到熟练掌握该项操作技能的目的。

First of all, the teacher will demonstrate and explain the general procedures for handling common problems on boarding, and prepare a certain number of common cases. Students are divided into groups of four and a group leader is selected to go to the teacher to draw the case. Each team member conducts simulations based on the extracted cases and takes on different identities (guests and staff) respectively. In the process of student simulation training, teachers provide guidance, and students repeatedly strengthen training. After group simulation training, a scenario is presented. Teachers and students, as well as among students themselves, conduct discussions and evaluations to achieve the goal of proficiently mastering this operational skill.

实训准备 Training Preparation

信息:相关案例及案例中的道具等。

Information: Relevant cases and props in cases, etc.

实训内容及操作标准 Training Content and Operating Standards

作为一名合格的邮轮登船部服务员应熟练掌握登船服务流程,能熟练地处理常见的登船问题。具体程序如下:

As a qualified attendant in the cruise boarding department, one should be proficient in the boarding service process and be able to handle common boarding problems skillfully. The specific procedures are as follows:

登船常见问题示例(Examples of Frequently Asked Questions about Boarding):

1.原本预定的普通舱房,登船后要求升级舱房。

The guest who originally booked an ordinary cabin requests to upgrade the cabin after boarding the ship.

2.邮轮船卡因宾客原因不慎丢失。

The cruise ship card was accidentally lost by the guest.

3.家庭游宾客带一名婴儿,需要婴儿床服务。

A family with a baby needs a crib service.

4.邮轮靠港时,宾客想邀请访客上船。

When the cruise ship docks at the port, guests wish to invite visitors to board the ship.

5.未到登船时间,宾客因个人原因申请提前登船。

Before the scheduled boarding time, guests apply for early boarding due to personal reasons.

6.宾客想携带私人轿车上船,并在靠岸时进行岸上自驾游。

Guests want to bring their private cars on board and go on a shore self-driving tour when the ship docks.

7.宾客想携带脚踏车上船,在邮轮甲板上骑行。

Guests want to bring their bicycles on board and ride them on the cruise ship's deck.

8.非盲人群体宾客想携带宠物上船。

Non-blind guests want to bring their pets on board.

9.大陆宾客到了台湾当地,想要自由行。

Mainland guests who arrive in Taiwan want to travel independently.

10.宾客因个人原因错过了登船时间,询问补救方案。

Guests missed the boarding time due to personal reasons and inquired about remedies.

登船常见问题处理程序(Procedures for Handling Frequently Asked Questions about Boarding):

1.需认真、耐心地听取(秉持高度的礼节礼貌,代表邮轮向宾客诚挚致歉并致谢)。

Listen carefully and patiently (upholding a high standard of courtesy and politeness, and sincerely apologize to the guests and express gratitude on behalf of the cruise ship).

2.仔细聆听具体内容(包括时间、地点、事件经过以及可能涉及的部门),并且要当着宾客的面进行详细记录。倘若宾客情绪较为激动,需想办法引导宾客前往合适的地点进行交谈。

Pay attention to the specific details (including the time, place, course of events and the departments that may be involved), and make detailed records in the presence of the guests. If the guests are rather emotional, find ways to guide the guests to a suitable place for a conversation.

3.需对宾客的遭遇表示理解,适时说出一些共情话语,让宾客切实感受到你对其处境的体谅。

One should show understanding of the guests' situation and seize the right moment to utter some empathetic words, enabling the guests to truly feel that you empathize with their circumstances.

4.在倾听宾客诉求的过程中,务必保持冷静。待明确事情缘由后,即刻做出准确判断。

When listening to the guests' requests, it is essential to remain calm. Once the cause has been ascertained, make an accurate judgment immediately.

5.当着宾客的面与相关部门取得联系,着手处理宾客的诉求。对于一时无法解决的问题,向宾客做出解释,并告知宾客即将采取的措施。

Contact the relevant departments in the presence of the guests and start handling the guests' requests. For issues that cannot be resolved immediately, provide explanations to the guests and inform them of the measures to be taken.

6.把宾客的诉求和意见传达给相关部门,以促使问题得到迅速解决。

Convey the guests' demands and opinions to the relevant departments to prompt the rapid resolution of problems.

7.对于极少数不讲道理的宾客,在处理时应做到维护国家及邮轮的利益。同时,态度需温和,语言与举止务必礼貌,并依据实际情况采取有效措施。

For a very small number of unreasonable guests, when handling the situation, it is essential to safeguard the interests of the country and the cruise ship. Meanwhile, the attitude should be amiable, the language and demeanor must be polite, and effective measures should be adopted according to the actual circumstances.

8.检查后续的处理结果。

Check the follow-up processing results.

9.宾客登船后可在适当时机回访,了解宾客感受。

After the guests board the ship, they can be interviewed about their feelings at an appropriate time.

10.收集宾客意见,通知相关部门,并录入宾客档案,以便在宾客下次到店时提供有针对性的服务,避免宾客再次提出相同诉求。

Collect guests' opinions, notify the relevant departments, and record them in the guest files. This enables us to provide targeted services when guests visit our establishment next time and avoid guests raising the same demands again.

登船常见问题处理图解
Illustration of the Handling of Frequently Asked Questions about Boarding

1.倾听诉求
Listen to the Appeal

2.记录诉求
Record the Appeal

3.情感共鸣
Emotional Resonance

4.理解意图
Understand the Intention

5.联系相关部门
Contact Relevant Departments

6.处理诉求
Handling Appeals

7.落实回访
Implement the Return Visit

8.记录在册
Record in the Book

实训任务考核指南
Training Task Assessment Guide

实训任务 Training Task	分值(分) Score（Points）	实际得分 Actual Score
仪容仪表、礼貌礼节 Grooming, Politeness and Etiquette	10	
案例模拟流程 Case Simulation Procedure	20	
案例处理质量 Quality of Case Handling	20	
案例处理熟练度 Proficiency of Case Handling	40	
案例处理结果 Case Handling Results	10	
【合计】 Total	100	

邮轮离船服务 项目 5
Cruise Disembarkation Service　Project 5

任务 1　邮轮离船服务
Mission 1
Cruise Disembarkation Service

实训目的
Training Objectives

通过教师对邮轮离船操作程序及要求的讲解,学生将全面掌握邮轮离船流程,涵盖宾客服务、行李托运、结账服务、安全检查以及离船指导等环节,从而确保宾客拥有顺畅、高效的离船体验。

Through the teacher's explanation of the operation procedures and requirements of cruise disembarkation, students will comprehensively master the disembarkation process of cruises, including guest service, luggage consignment, check-out procedures, security checks, and disembarkation guidance, ensuring a smooth and efficient disembarkation experience for guests.

实训方法
Training Method

通过课堂讲解与模拟操作相结合的方式,学生将借助模拟离船场景,演练从接待宾客到宾客最终离船的完整流程。在此过程中,教师会在一旁进行指导并给予反馈。

Combining classroom instruction with simulated operations, students will practice the entire process from guests reception to guests' final disembarkation through simulated disembarkation scenarios. In the process, teachers will be on the side to provide guidance and feedback.

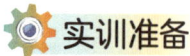

实训准备
Training Preparation

模拟离船等候区、模拟安全检查点和离船出口、行李牌等。

Simulated disembarkation waiting area, simulated security checkpoint, disembarkation exit, luggage tags, etc.

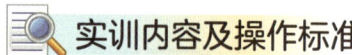

实训内容及操作标准
Training Content and Operating Standards

作为一名合格的邮轮乘务人员,需要熟练掌握邮轮宾客的离船操作程序。具体包括:学习如何以友好且专业的方式迎接离船宾客;练习如何帮助宾客了解行李离船手续,确保行李安全、及时地运送到指定地点;学习如何向宾客提供离船信息,例如出口位置、交通安排等,以此确保宾客顺利离船,并在此过程中为宾客提供必要的信息和帮助。具体程序如下:

As a qualified cruise crew member, you need to be proficient in the disembarkation procedures for cruise guests. Specifically, it includes learning how to greet disembarking guests in a friendly and professional manner; practicing how to assist guests in understanding the luggage disembarkation formalities and ensuring that luggage is safely and promptly transported to the designated location; learning how to provide disembarkation information to guests, such as the exit location, transportation arrangements, etc., thereby ensuring that guests can disembark smoothly and providing them with necessary information and assistance during the process. The specific procedures are as follows:

邮轮离船的程序(Cruise Disembarkation Procedure):

1.离船指南发放:在宾客离船前一天,向其发放离船指南。指南内容应涵盖离船当日早餐的时间与地点,以及不同甲板的相关信息。

Issuance of Disembarkation Guide: Issue the disembarkation guide to guests one day before they disembark. The guide should cover the time and place of breakfast on the day of disembarkation as well as information related to different decks.

2.行李牌发放与核对:为即将离船的宾客发放行李牌,并指导他们完成行李牌的登记工作。

Issuance and Verification of Luggage Tags: Issue luggage tags to guests who are about to disembark and guide them to complete the registration of the luggage tags.

3.扣款操作:于后台执行扣款流程。首先从宾客的预授权中扣除相应款项,若预授权额度不足,则从其信用卡账户中扣除剩余部分。

Deduction Process: The deduction process is carried out in the background. First, the corresponding amount is deducted from the guests' pre-authorization. If the pre-authorization amount is insufficient, the remaining amount is deducted from the credit card account.

4.宾客引导:将离船宾客引导至指定的离船等候区域。

Guest Guidance: Guide disembarking guests to the designated disembarkation waiting area.

5.应急处理:学习应对离船过程中可能出现的紧急状况,例如宾客物品遗失、协助行李寻回等情况。

Emergency Handling: Learn how to handle emergency situations that may occur during the disembarkation process, such as guests' lost items and assistance with luggage retrieval.

实训任务考核指南
Training Task Assessment Guide

实训任务 Training Task	分值(分) Score (Points)	实际得分 Actual Score
仪容仪表、礼貌礼节 Grooming, Politeness and Etiquette	10	
离船指南通知及流程解释 Notification and Explanation of Disembarkation Information	20	
行李牌填写 Fill in the Luggage Tags	20	
离船流程引导 Guidance on Disembarkation Procedures	40	
应急情况处理 Emergency Situation Handling	10	
【合计】 Total	100	

模块 3
礼宾服务

Module 3
Concierge Service

项目 1　行李服务
Project 1　Luggage Service

任务 1　登船行李托运
Mission 1　Luggage Check-in for Boarding

实训目的 Training Objectives

通过教师对邮轮登船行李托运程序及操作要求的讲解,以及学生对登船行李托运技能的训练,让学生了解并掌握邮轮登船行李托运的操作程序、操作标准与操作要领,以达到熟知操作程序和操作规范的训练要求。

Through the teacher's explanation of the procedures and operation requirements for cruise ship boarding luggage consignment, as well as the students' training in boarding luggage consignment skills, the students will be enabled to understand and master the operation procedures, operation standards and key operation points of cruise ship boarding luggage consignment, so as to meet the training requirements of being well-versed in operation procedures and operation norms.

实训方法 Training Method

首先,教师进行示范讲解,随后学生开展动手操作训练。在学生操作训练期间,教师予以指导,学生通过反复练习强化技能,从而达到熟练掌握该项操作技能的目的。

Firstly, the teacher conducts a demonstration and gives an explanation. Subsequently, the students carry out hands-on operation training. During the students' operation training, the teacher provides guidance. The students reinforce their skills through repeated practice so as to achieve the goal of proficiently mastering the operation skills.

实训准备
Training Preparation

行李箱、登船行李牌、行李车、安检仪器等。

Luggage, boarding luggage tag, luggage cart, security inspection equipment, etc.

实训内容及操作标准
Training Content and Operating Standards

作为一名合格的邮轮工作人员,不仅要具备扎实的邮轮服务理论知识,更重要的是要熟练掌握各项实操技能。登船行李托运的具体程序如下:

As a qualified cruise staff member, not only should one possess solid theoretical knowledge of cruise services, but more importantly, one should proficiently master various practical skills. The specific procedures for boarding luggage consignment are as follows:

登船行李托运的程序(Luggage Check-in for Boarding Procedure):

1.准备行李:在登船前,整理好需要托运的行李。务必保证行李内未携带任何违禁品或危险品。

Prepare the luggage: Before boarding, prepare the luggage to be checked. Make sure your luggage does not contain any contraband or dangerous goods.

2.领取行李条:在登船大厅或指定地点,向工作人员领取行李条。行李条上一般会印有您的姓名、房间号等信息。

Collect luggage tags: Collect luggage tags from the staff at the boarding hall or the designated place. The luggage tag is usually printed with your name, room number and other information.

3.粘贴行李条:将行李条撕下,牢固地粘贴在行李上,方便工作人员准确识别并运送行李。

Attach the luggage tags: Tear off the luggage tags and attach them firmly to the luggage so that the staff can accurately identify and transport the luggage.

4.托运行李:把贴好行李条的行李交给工作人员办理托运。托运时,请出示有效的登船证明和身份证明。

Check-in the luggage: Give the luggage with luggage tags to the staff for checking. Please be sure to present valid proof of boarding and identification.

5.获取行李牌与收据:工作人员会在行李上粘贴行李牌,并提供相应的行李收据作为凭证。请妥善保管行李收据，以便日后查询行李状态。

Obtain Luggage Tags and Receipts: The staff will attach a luggage tag to the luggage and provide the corresponding luggage receipt as proof. Keep your luggage receipts safe so you can check your luggage status if needed.

6.行李送达：通常情况下，登船后，工作人员会将行李送至指定客舱。请注意收听广播或向工作人员询问，了解行李送达的时间及方式。

Luggage Delivery: In general, after boarding, the luggage will be taken to the designated cabin by the staff. Listen to the radio or consult the staff to find out when and how your luggage will be delivered.

7.特殊情况处理：若登船时选择自行携带行李，但登船后发现行李不便携带或需要临时寄存，可向工作人员咨询是否有行李寄存服务。船上一般设有行李寄存处，您可将行李寄存于此，并在需要时取回。

Handling Special Situations: If you choose to carry your luggage when boarding, but find it inconvenient to carry or need temporary storage after boarding, please ask the staff whether there is luggage storage service. There is usually a luggage storage on board where luggage can be stored and retrieved when needed.

邮轮行李托运违禁物品
Prohibited Items of Luggage Check-in for Boarding

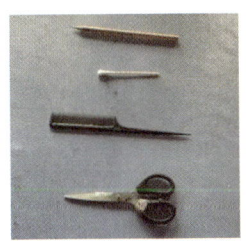

1.尖锐物品
Sharp Objects

2.体育棍棒
Sporting Sticks

3.禁用化学品
Prohibited Chemicals

4.压缩气筒
Compressed Gas Barrel

5.民爆器材
Civil Explosive Equipment

6.工具
Tools

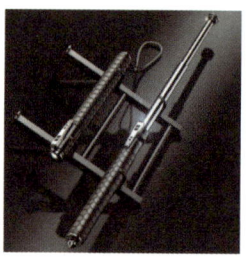

7.枪支武器　　　　　　　8.武术及防身用品　　　　　9 易燃物品
Firearms　　　　　　　**Martial Arts and**　　　　**Flammable Materials**
　　　　　　　　　　　　Self-defense Articles

实训任务考核指南
Training Task Assessment Guide

实训任务 Training Task	分值(分) Score (Points)	实际得分 Actual Score
仪容仪表、礼貌礼节 Grooming, Politeness and Etiquette	10	
操作程序 Operating Procedure	20	
操作动作 Operating Action	20	
操作质量 Operating Quality	40	
操作时间 Operating Time	10	
【合计】 Total	100	

任务 2 离船行李托运
Mission 2
Disembarkation Luggage Consignment

实训目的
Training Objectives

通过教师对邮轮离船行李托运程序及操作要求的讲解,以及学生针对离船行李托运技能展开的训练,使学生得以了解并掌握邮轮离船行李托运的操作程序、操作标准和操作要领,从而达到熟知操作程序与操作规范的训练要求。

Through the teacher's explanation of the procedures and operational requirements for cruise ship disembarkation luggage consignment, as well as the students' training in disembarkation luggage consignment skills, the students will be enabled to understand and master the operating procedures, operating standards and key operating points of cruise ship disembarkation luggage consignment, thus meeting the training requirements of being well-versed in the operating procedures and operational norms.

实训方法
Training Method

首先,教师进行示范讲解;随后,学生展开动手操作训练。在学生操作训练期间,教师予以指导,学生通过反复练习强化技能,进而达到熟练掌握该项操作技能的目的。

Firstly, the teacher conducts a demonstration and gives an explanation. Subsequently, the students carry out hands-on operation training. During the students' operation training, the teacher provides guidance. The students reinforce their skills through repeated practice so as to achieve the goal of proficiently mastering the operation skills.

实训准备
Training Preparation

行李箱、登船行李牌、行李车等。
Luggage, boarding luggage tags, luggage carts, etc.

实训内容及操作标准
Training Content and Operating Standards

作为一名合格的邮轮工作人员,不仅要具备扎实的邮轮服务理论知识,更为关键的是要熟练掌握各项实操技能。离船行李托运的具体程序如下:

As a qualified cruise staff member, not only should one possess solid theoretical knowledge of cruise services, but more importantly, one should proficiently master various practical skills. The specific procedures for disembarkation luggage consignment are as follows:

离船行李托运的程序(Disembarkation Luggage Consignment Procedure):

1.准备行李(Pack Your Luggage)

提前整理好需托运的行李,务必保证行李符合邮轮公司在尺寸、重量等方面的规定。同时,取出诸如护照、钱包、手机、充电器等需要随身携带的物品。

Pack your checked luggage in advance to ensure they meet cruise line regulations regarding size, weight limits. Take out items that you need to carry with you, such as your passport, wallet, cell phone, and phone charger.

2.行李牌(Luggage Tags)

使用邮轮公司提供的行李牌,或者自行准备清晰易辨的行李条,务必清楚标注姓名、房间号等关键信息。仔细检查行李条粘贴是否牢固、有无破损,防止在运输途中脱落或损坏。

Use the luggage tags provided by the cruise line or prepare your own clear-legible luggage tags, ensuring that key information such as name and room number is clearly marked. Carefully check whether the luggage tags are firmly attached and free of damage to prevent them from falling off or getting damaged during transportation.

3.行李归类(Luggage Classification)

根据邮轮公司的要求,将行李按照指定的区域或编号进行分类。如果邮轮公司提供不同颜色的行李牌,按照标签颜色将行李归类。

Luggage is sorted by designated area or number as requested by the cruise line. If the cruise line offers luggage tags in different colors, sort your luggage according to the color of the tags.

4.行李托运(Luggage Check)

在规定的时间内,将行李送至邮轮公司指定的行李托运处。与工作人员确认行李信息,确保行李被正确托运。

Deliver your luggage to the luggage drop off designated by the cruise line within the specified time. Verify luggage information with staff to ensure that luggage is checked correctly.

5. 领取行李收据(Get Your Luggage Receipt)

在行李托运后,务必向工作人员领取行李收据,作为领取行李的凭证。

After the luggage is checked in, be sure to collect the luggage receipt from the staff as proof of luggage claim.

6. 离船(Get off the Ship)

完成行李托运后,按照邮轮公司的指示办理离船手续。如有需要,可以向工作人员了解行李预计送达的时间和地点。

After your luggage is checked in, follow the instructions of the cruise line for disembankation. If necessary, you can ask the staff to find out when and where the luggage is expected to arrive.

7. 提取行李(Luggage Claim)

抵达港口后,根据邮轮公司的指示前往行李提取区。出示行李收据和船票等证件,领取自己的行李。

Upon arrival at the port, proceed to the luggage claim area as directed by the cruise line. Show your luggage receipt and cruise ticket and other documents to collect your luggage.

8. 特殊情况处理(Handling Special Cases)

如果在行李提取时发现行李丢失或损坏,请立即与邮轮公司或港口工作人员联系,并按照相关程序进行索赔。

If you find your luggage lost or damaged during luggage claim, contact the cruise line or port staff immediately and follow the relevant procedures to make a claim.

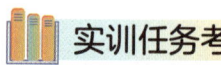

实训任务考核指南
Training Task Assessment Guide

实训任务 Training Task	分值（分） Score（Points）	实际得分 Actual Score
仪容仪表、礼貌礼节 Grooming, Politeness and Etiquette	10	
操作程序 Operating Procedure	20	
操作动作 Operating Action	20	
操作质量 Operating Quality	40	
操作时间 Operating Time	10	
【合计】 Total	100	

贵宾服务 项目2
VIP Service Project 2

任务1 了解邮轮贵宾服务
Mission 1 Knowing Cruise VIP Services

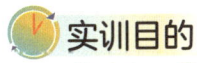
实训目的 Training Objectives

通过教师对邮轮贵宾服务的基本内容、服务流程及要求的讲解,以及学生对邮轮贵宾服务接待流程的学习和模拟训练,学生能够了解并掌握贵宾服务的接待流程与服务规范,从而达到熟知服务流程与服务规范的训练目标。

Through the teachers' explanation of the basic content, service processes and requirements of cruise VIP services and the students' learning and simulation training on the reception processes of cruise VIP services, students can understand and master the reception procedures and standards of cruise VIP services, and meet the training objectives of being well-acquainted with service procedures and standards.

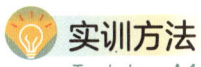
实训方法 Training Method

首先,教师梳理并讲解相关知识点,随后学生以小组为单位开展角色扮演训练。在学生小组练习期间,教师进行指导与纠正,学生通过反复强化训练,从而达成熟练掌握该项操作技能的目标。

Firstly, the teacher sorts out and explains the relevant knowledge points. Subsequently, the students carry out role-playing exercises in groups. During the students' group practice, the teacher provides guidance and corrects errors, and the students repeatedly strengthen their training to achieve the goal of proficiently mastering the operational skills.

实训准备 Training Preparation

VIP宾客信息卡、邮轮日报、房卡、账单、邮轮综合实训室等。

VIP guest information card, cruise daily, room card, bill, cruise integrated training room, etc.

实训内容及操作标准 Training Content and Operating Standards

国际邮轮的贵宾服务是一种经过升级的服务体验,旨在为宾客提供更为尊贵、舒适且便利的旅行服务。国际邮轮的贵宾服务通常涵盖专属的贵宾套房、私人管家服务、优先登船与离船特权,以及专属的餐饮和娱乐设施等。贵宾套房一般具备更宽敞的空间、更奢华的装修以及更舒适的设施,从而为宾客打造高品质的住宿体验。私人管家服务能够为宾客提供个性化服务,例如行程规划、餐厅预订、纪念品购置等。优先登船和离船特权可使宾客免去排队等候,节省时间。专属的餐饮和娱乐设施能让宾客在船上拥有更为丰富多彩的体验。

International cruise VIP service is an upgraded service experience designed to provide guests with more distinguished, comfortable and convenient travel services. International cruise VIP services typically include exclusive VIP suites, private butler services, priority boarding and disembarkation, exclusive dining and entertainment facilities, and more. VIP suites usually have more spacious accommodation, more luxurious decorations and more comfortable amenities to provide guests with a high-quality accommodation experience. Private butler services can provide personalized services for guests, such as arranging trips, making restaurant reservations, and purchasing souvenirs. Priority boarding and disembarkation allows guests to avoid queues and save time. Exclusive dining and entertainment facilities allow guests to enjoy a more colorful experience on board.

贵宾服务属于邮轮礼宾服务的范畴。作为一名合格的礼宾员,不仅要掌握扎实的礼宾服务理论知识,还需熟知贵宾服务的内容与要求,通过更为细致、贴心的服务打动宾客,为其带来极致的邮轮旅行体验。贵宾服务流程涵盖接待前的准备工作、登船服务、航行期间服务以及离船服务这四个部分。具体程序如下:

VIP services is a part of the cruise concierge service. As a qualified concierge, in addition to having a solid theoretical knowledge of concierge service, one/they should also understand the content and requirements of VIP services, to impress guests with more meticulous and attentive service, enabling them to enjoy the ultimate cruise travel experience. The process includes four parts: pre-reception preparations, boarding service, in-cruise service, and disembarkation service. The specific procedures are as follows:

接待前的准备工作(Preparation before Reception):

1.了解 VIP 宾客的相关信息,内容涵盖:姓名、国籍、身份、年龄、性别、风俗习惯、宗教信仰、健康状况、生活习惯、接待标准以及日程安排等。同时,要充分学习并熟悉各项接待服务程序与细节。

Understand the relevant information of VIP guests, including name, nationality, identity, age, gender, customs, religious beliefs, health status, living habits, reception standards, and schedule, etc. Fully learn and get familiar with various reception service procedures and details.

2.与各部门提前做好沟通协调工作。依据宾客的具体情况,协同客房部确定 VIP 宾客的入住房间并完成相关布置;同时,与餐饮部妥善安排好 VIP 宾客在船期间的用餐事宜,以此确保各项接待任务能够顺利完成。

Communicate with all departments in advance. According to the specific situation of the guests, work with the housekeeping department to determine the rooms for VIP guests and complete the relevant decorations. At the same time, coordinate with the Food and Beverage Department to properly arrange the dining for VIP guests during the cruise, so as to ensure the smooth completion of all reception tasks.

登船服务(Boarding Service):

1.在邮轮登船口等候,迎接宾客并进行自我介绍。
Wait at the boarding gate to greet guests and introduce yourself.
2.安排宾客优先办理登船手续。
Arrange priority check-in for guests.
3.将宾客送至客房。在此过程中,为宾客介绍服务设施、服务项目和行程。
Escort guests to their rooms. In this process, introduce the service facilities, service items and itinerary to the guests.

航行期间服务(Service during Cruise):

1.与宾客沟通行程安排,协助宾客完成餐厅预订或活动报名。同时,依据日程安排表,提前在宾客客舱门口等候。

Communicate with guests about the itinerary, assist them in making reservations at restaurants or for activities, and wait in advance at the doors of guests' cabins according to the schedule.

2.当宾客外出用餐或参加活动时,需全程陪同前往。引路时,应走在宾客左前方约 1 米处。遇到转弯处或坡坎,要及时回头向宾客示意,并提醒他们留意脚下安全。乘坐电梯时,要用一只手按住电梯门的感应槽,邀请宾客先进入电梯,随后自己进入电梯并靠近控制台站立,以便于操作电梯。离开电梯时,让宾客先行,然后迅速跟上,继续在前方为宾客指引路线。

When guests go out for meals or to participate in activities, accompany them and walk about 1 meter in front of and to the left of the guests. When encountering a turn or a slope, turn around and gesture to the guests, reminding them to watch their step. When taking the elevator, use one hand to press and hold the sensor of the elevator door, invite the guests to enter the elevator first, and then enter the elevator yourself and stand near the control panel for easy operation. When exiting the elevator, let the guests go first, then quickly catch up and continue to lead the way in front.

3.在宾客用餐或观看表演期间,应在宾客座位附近随时待命,密切留意宾客需求,同时与现场服务员保持紧密沟通,以确保宾客的各类需求都能得到及时满足。

When guests are dining or watching performances, remain on standby near their seats, closely monitor their needs, and maintain close communication with the on-site wait staff to ensure that all their needs are promptly met.

4.用餐结束后,需护送宾客返回房间。在途中,可适时询问宾客对用餐体验的感受,从而为其提供更优质的后续服务。

After the meal, escort the guests back to their rooms. On the way, appropriately inquire about their dining experience to offer more excellent follow-up services.

5.在宾客上岸游览前,需提前与导游取得联系,确认宾客所乘坐的车(船)编号。当地接人员登船后,及时通知宾客下船,并一路陪同宾客到达车(船)处。在此过程中,要向宾客送上游览愉快的祝福,直至车(船)驶离后再返回。

Before the guests go ashore, contact the guide in advance to confirm the guests' vehicle or vessel number. Once the local reception staff board the ship, promptly notify the guests to disembark and accompany them all the way to the vehicle or vessel. During this process, extend good wishes for a pleasant tour to the guests and return only after the vehicle or vessel departs.

6.在宾客返回船上前,需提前前往宾客下车(船)的地点等候。

Before the guests return to the ship, the concierge should arrive at the guests' disembarkation point (for vehicle or vessel) in advance and wait.

7.在服务期间,需时刻留意宾客的需求与情绪变化,保证服务周到入微。

During the service, the concierge should constantly monitor the needs and emotional changes of the guests to ensure that the service is comprehensive and attentive.

离船服务(Disembarkation Service):

1.从财务部收款人员处收集整理好宾客的消费账单,随后带至宾客房间,与宾客逐项仔细核对。在确认账单准确无误后,安排宾客优先前往前台完成付款事宜。

Take the collected and sorted consumption bills from the collection staff of the finance department to the guests' room and check them item by item with the guests. After confirming that the bill is correct, arrange for the guests to complete the payment at the front desk.

2.引导宾客通过VIP专用通道下船,一直陪同至岸上,随后向宾客致以诚挚的告别。

Guide guests to disembark through the VIP channel and escort them to the shore, then bid them a sincere farewell.

<h3 style="text-align:center">贵宾服务步骤图解
Step Diagram of VIP Service</h3>

1.（接待前的准备工作）
Preparation before Reception

2.（登船服务）
Boarding Service

3.（航行期间服务）
Service during Cruise

4.（离船服务）
Disembarkation Service

以小组为单位，运用本节课所学知识，通过角色扮演来呈现以下情境。

Work in groups and role play the following scenario according to the knowledge learned in this lesson.

情境：一对年过六旬的夫妻预订了某知名邮轮公司的豪华套房，打算通过一次难忘的邮轮之旅来纪念他们的结婚纪念日。邮轮礼宾服务团队为他们进行了精心筹备，并且在整个过程中凭借高品质服务，让宾客十分满意。

Scenario: A couple over 60 booked a luxury suite from a well-known cruise line to commemorate their wedding anniversary with an unforgettable cruise trip. The cruise concierge team made elaborate preparations for them and delighted the guests with high-quality service throughout the whole process.

实训任务考核指南
Training Task Assessment Guide

实训任务 Training Task	分值(分) Score (Points)	实际得分 Actual Score
仪容仪表、礼貌礼节 Grooming, Politeness and Etiquette	10	
操作程序 Operating Procedure	20	
操作动作 Operating Action	20	
操作质量 Operating Quality	40	
操作时间 Operating Time	10	
【合计】 Total	100	

礼宾服务常见问题处理 项目 3

Common Problems Handling in Concierge Services

Project 3

任务 1　常见案例分享

Mission 1

Common Case Sharing

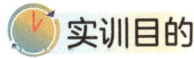
实训目的 *Training Objectives*

教师通过讲解邮轮礼宾服务中常见问题的处理办法，并分享常见案例，让学生对礼宾服务的要求和标准有了更深刻的理解，同时掌握礼宾服务中常见问题的处理流程与方法，以达到能够正确处理礼宾服务常见问题的训练要求。

Through the teacher's explanation of common problem-solving methods in cruise concierge service and the sharing of common cases, students gain a deeper understanding of the requirements and standards of concierge service, and can master the process and methods of handling common problems in concierge service, so as to meet the training requirements for correctly handling common problems in concierge service.

实训方法 *Training Method*

首先，教师进行案例分享与讲解，助力学生了解礼宾服务中常见问题的处理方法。接着，教师给出礼宾服务案例让学生思考，要求学生以小组形式展开讨论，得出问题的解决方案,并通过角色扮演将其展示出来。在学生表演结束后,教师予以点评。随后,学生进行反复强化训练,直至熟练掌握该项操作技能。

First, the teacher shares cases and gives explanations to help students understand how to deal with common problems in concierge service. Then, the teacher gives several common cases of concierge service for students to think about, and asks students to discuss in groups and come up with solutions to the problems, and then show them through role-playing. After the students' performance, the teacher makes comments, and the students repeatedly strengthen the training until they master the operation skill proficiently.

实训准备
Training Preparation

邮轮综合实训室。
Cruise integrated training room.

实训内容及操作标准
Training Content and Operating Standards

一、案例分析
Analyze the Following Two Cases

案例一:王先生在登船前办理了行李托运,登船进入房间后,却迟迟未等到自己的行李。焦急的王先生向礼宾员询问行李去向。礼宾员小李立刻安抚王先生,详细询问其行李箱的特征,同时将这一情况汇报给前台经理。经相关工作人员积极寻找,原来是行李员疏忽,把王先生的行李遗忘在了行李运输车上。在搜寻行李期间,小李始终陪伴在王先生身旁,一边安慰王先生别着急,一边将搜寻进度及时告知他。最终,行李员把找到的行李箱送至王先生房间,并诚恳致歉,获得了王先生的谅解。

Case 1: Mr. Wang checked his luggage before boarding the ship. However, after boarding and entering his room, he waited in vain for his luggage. Anxious, Mr. Wang asked the concierge about the whereabouts of his luggage. The concierge, Xiao Li, immediately soothed Mr. Wang and inquired in detail about the features of his suitcase. Meanwhile, he reported the situation to the front desk manager. Through the active search of the relevant staff, it turned out that Mr. Wang's luggage had been left on the luggage transport vehicle due to the porter's negligence. During the luggage-searching period, Xiao Li accompanied Mr. Wang all the time, reassuring him not to worry and keeping him informed of the search progress. Finally, the porter delivered the found suitcase to Mr. Wang's room, apologized sincerely, and gained Mr. Wang's forgiveness.

案例二:陈女士和她的工作伙伴因商务洽谈登船,她打算预定船上的会议室以及举办商务晚宴。于是,陈女士向负责接待她上船的礼宾员咨询预定相关事宜。当时,礼宾员正忙于手头事务,便直接把邮轮商务中心和餐厅的电话告知了陈女士。陈女士只好亲自打电话完成了会议室和晚宴的预定。然而,作为邮轮常客的她,心里对此感到不太满意。

Case 2: Ms. Chen and her working partners boarded the cruise for business negotiations. She intended to reserve the meeting room and arrange a business dinner on board. So she inquired with the concierge who was responsible for receiving her about the reservation procedures. The concierge was so busy dealing with other tasks that he simply gave her the phone numbers of the business center and the restaurant. Ms. Chen had to call to make reservations for the meeting room and dinner herself. However, as a frequent cruiser, she felt rather displeased about this.

分析(Analysis)

案例一:在登船过程中,若出现宾客托运的行李丢失情况,通常的解决方法如下:

Case 1: During the boarding process, if the guest's checked luggage is lost, the general solution is:

1.第一时间安抚宾客情绪,并详细了解行李相关情况。

Comfort the guests' emotions immediately and understand the details related to the luggage thoroughly.

2.迅速向上级领导进行报告。

Report to the superiors promptly.

3.全面调查行李丢失或错拿的具体情况,积极采取有效措施找回行李。

Conduct a comprehensive investigation into the specific situation of luggage loss or misappropriation, and actively take effective measures to retrieve the luggage.

4.为宾客及时提供必要的替代物品,以解燃眉之急。

Provide the guests with necessary substitute items in a timely manner to relieve their urgent needs.

5.持续向宾客实时通报行李查找的最新进展。

Continuously update the guests on the latest progress of the luggage search in real-time.

6.在成功解决行李问题后,做好后续跟进工作,确保宾客满意。

After successfully resolving the luggage issue, do a good job in the follow-up work to ensure the guests' satisfaction.

案例一中礼宾员第一时间安抚了宾客的情绪,并通过问询行李的基本特征为后面的找寻行李做好铺垫,通过向前台经理汇报,让各个相关人员和部门立刻参与到搜寻中,为及时找回行李创造了条件。等待行李期间,他通过向宾客更新找寻进度,缓解宾客的焦虑,并让他感到问题正在得到解决。行李被找到,他立即通知宾客,并安排将行李送至宾客的房间。同时,对于给宾客带来的不便表示歉意,并感谢他的理解和耐心。通过这些步骤,邮轮礼宾员妥善处理宾客行李未到达房间的问题,确保宾客的满意度和舒适度。同时,这也体现了邮轮服务团队的高效和专业性。

In Case 1, the concierge soothed the guest's emotions right away. By inquiring about the basic features of the luggage, he paved the way for the subsequent search. After reporting to the front desk manager, relevant personnel and departments were promptly engaged in the search, which created favorable conditions for retrieving the luggage in a timely manner. During the waiting period, he alleviated the guest's anxiety by keeping him updated on the search progress, making him feel that the problem was being addressed. Once the luggage was located, he immediately informed the guest and arranged to have the luggage delivered to his rooms. Meanwhile, he apologized for the inconvenience caused to the guest and expressed gratitude for his understanding and patience. Through these steps, the cruise concierge properly dealt with the issue of the guest' sluggage not reaching their rooms, ensuring guest satisfaction and comfort. This also demonstrates the efficiency and professionalism of the cruise service team.

案例二：根据材料，陈女士因商务洽谈登船，且是邮轮的常客。由此可推测，她是一位追求高品质旅行体验的宾客，极有可能是享有贵宾服务礼遇的 VIP 宾客。当邮轮 VIP 宾客希望预订会议室和餐厅时，专属的私人管家应采取以下步骤来满足他们的需求：

Case 2：According to the materials, Ms. Chen boarded the cruise ship for business negotiations and is a frequent cruiser. It can be inferred that she is a guest who pursues a high-quality travel experience and is likely a VIP guest enjoying VIP service. When cruise VIP guests wish to reserve meeting rooms and restaurants, the dedicated personal butler should take the following steps to meet their needs：

1.明确需求：详细了解宾客预订会议的时间、时长、参会人数，以及是否有其他特殊需求；对于餐厅预订，了解宾客对就餐环境、食物的要求，有无特殊偏好或忌口等。

Clarify the requirements：Thoroughly understand the time, duration, number of participants of the meeting the guest intends to book, as well as any other special requirements. Regarding restaurant reservations, find out the guest's requirements for the dining environment, food, and whether there are any special preferences or dietary restrictions.

2.给出方案：依据宾客需求，提供多种不同方案供宾客挑选。

Provide options：Based on the guest's needs, offer multiple different options for the guest to select from.

3.完成预订：宾客选定方案后，及时与邮轮相关部门落实预订事宜，并进行确认。

Complete the reservation：Once the guest has made a choice, promptly coordinate with the relevant cruise departments to finalize the reservation and confirm it.

4.提前筹备：在预订时间前，再次检查各项服务细节是否落实到位，设施设备能否正常运转。

Prepare in advance：Before the reserved time, double-check whether all service details have been properly implemented and whether the facilities and equipment are in normal operation.

5.跟进反馈：会议或就餐结束后，主动与宾客沟通，了解其对安排及服务的满意度，收集反馈意见，助力进一步提升服务质量。

Follow-up and feedback：After the meeting or meal, take the initiative to communicate with the guests, understand their satisfaction with the arrangements and services, and collect feedback to contribute to further improving the service quality.

在这个案例中，礼宾员并未遵循上述服务流程进行操作，而是直接让陈女士自行打电话预订会议室和餐厅。这一做法使得宾客产生了不被重视的感觉,严重影响了宾客的体验,进而对邮轮的整体印象和满意度大打折扣。

The concierge in this case did not follow the above-mentioned service procedures. Instead, he/she directly asked Ms. Chen to make phone calls to book the meeting room and the restaurant by herself. This approach made the guest feel unvalued and significantly impaired the guest's experience, thus greatly reducing the guest's overall impression of and satisfaction with the cruise.

二、小组任务
Group Task

以小组为单位,对以下两个情境展开分析,提出具体的解决办法,并通过角色扮演的形式予以展示。

Work in groups to analyze the following two situations. Put forward specific solutions and present them through role-playing.

情境一:一位宾客登船后不久,向礼宾员反映自己还有一件行李迟迟未送达,他怀疑是行李中携带的电热水壶未能通过海关安检所致。假设你是这位礼宾员,你会如何处理?

Scenario 1: Shortly after boarding the ship, a guest reports to the concierge that one of his pieces of luggage has not been delivered yet. He suspects that it is due to an electric kettle in his luggage failing to pass the customs security check. Suppose you are the concierge, how would you handle this situation?

情境二:某知名豪华邮轮公司即将接待一位来自中东的贵宾。假设你是负责接待这位宾客的礼宾专员,你会做哪些准备工作?

Scenario 2: A renowned luxury cruise company is on the verge of receiving a VIP guest from the Middle East. Suppose you are the concierge in charge of receiving this guest, what preparations would you make?

实训任务考核指南
Training Task Assessment Guide

实训任务 Training Task	分值(分) Score (Points)	实际得分 Actual Score
仪容仪表、礼貌礼节 Grooming, Politeness and Etiquette	10	
操作程序 Operating Procedure	20	
操作动作 Operating Action	20	
操作质量 Operating Quality	40	
操作时间 Operating Time	10	
【合计】 Total	100	

模块 4
前台接待服务

Module 4
Reception Service

前台接待 项目 1
Reception Project 1

任务 1 认识邮轮前台
Mission 1
The Introduction of Cruise Reception Desk

邮轮前台是邮轮上负责接待、咨询并为宾客提供服务的重要部门(见图4-1和图4-2)。在不同的邮轮公司中,其岗位设置和名称可能存在差异,常见的称谓有 Receptionist(接待员)、Guest Service Associate(GSA,宾客服务专员)、Guest Service Officer(GSO,宾客服务主管)等。邮轮前台通常位于邮轮的主入口或大厅区域,是宾客登船后首先接触到的服务点。前台工作人员在邮轮与宾客之间扮演着桥梁角色,为宾客提供从入住登记、接待咨询、投诉处理到离船等一系列服务。工作人员需具备良好的业务能力、沟通能力、团队协作精神以及应变能力,以应对邮轮上复杂多变的工作环境。

The cruise reception desk is an important department on the cruise ship, responsible for receiving guests, providing consultation services, and offering assistance to them (see Figure 4-1 and Figure 4-2). The job positions and their names may vary among different cruise companies. Common titles include Receptionist, Guest Service Associate (GSA), and Guest Service Officer (GSO). Typically, the cruise reception desk is situated at the main entrance or in the lobby area of the cruise ship, serving as the first service point that guests come into contact with after boarding. The staff at the cruise reception desk act as a bridge between the cruise ship and the guests, offering a range of services such as check-in, handling reception inquiries, dealing with complaints, and assisting with the disembarkation process. It is essential for the staff to possess excellent professional skills, strong communication abilities, a spirit of teamwork, and the capacity to adapt, in order to manage the complex and ever-changing working environment on the cruise ship.

图 4-1　邮轮前台(1)

Figure 4-1　Cruise Reception Desk(1)

图 4-2　邮轮前台(2)

Figure 4-2　Cruise Reception Desk(2)

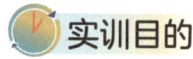

实训目的　Training Objectives

教师讲解邮轮前台的主要职责以及办理入住、退房的基本流程,学生通过模拟场景进行演练。借此,学生能够掌握操作程序、操作标准与操作要领,达成熟知操作程序与操作规范的训练要求。

The teacher explains the main responsibilities of the cruise reception desk as well as the basic check-in and check-out procedures. Then, the students conduct drills through simulated scenarios. Through this process, the students are able to master the operating procedures, standards, and key points, thus meeting the training requirements of being familiar with the operating procedures and norms.

实训方法　Training Method

首先,教师进行示范讲解。随后,学生开展模拟场景演练。在学生演练期间,教师予以指导,学生通过反复强化训练,从而达到熟练掌握该项操作技能的目的。

First, the teacher gives a demonstration and explanation. Subsequently, the students carry out simulated-scene drills. During the students' drills, the teacher provides guidance. Through repeated intensive training, the students can achieve the goal of mastering the operation skills proficiently.

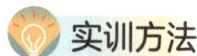

实训准备　Training Preparation

前台接待台、电脑、入住登记表、退房结账单、房卡、滚珠笔、邮轮服务指南手册等。

Reception desk, computer, check-in form, check-out bill, room card, rollerball pen, cruise service guide manual, etc.

实训内容及操作标准
Training Content and Operating Standards

作为一名合格的邮轮前台员工,除了要具备扎实的前台接待理论知识外,更为关键的是熟练掌握前台主要业务,如办理入住、退房等操作技能。具体操作程序如下:

As a qualified cruise reception desk staff member, apart from possessing solid theoretical knowledge of front desk reception, it is even more crucial to proficiently master the operational skills of key front desk services, such as check-in and check-out procedures. The specific operating procedures are as follows:

办理入住的程序(Procedure of Check-in):

1.主动引导宾客前往前台办理入住登记手续。

Proactively guide guests to the front desk to go through the check-in formalities.

2.办理入住手续时,宾客需提交相关证件,如护照、身份证等。工作人员认真核对证件是否齐全、有效后,填写相关表格信息。

When guests check-in, they need to submit relevant documents, such as passports, ID cards, etc. The staff should carefully check whether the documents are complete and valid and then fill in the relevant form information.

3.收到现金支付或绑定信用卡支付的押金后,宾客需在押金单或信用卡预授权单上签字确认。

After receiving the deposit either in cash or by credit card binding, guests need to sign the deposit slip or the credit card pre-authorization slip for confirmation.

4.为宾客分配房间并发放房卡。需要注意的是,宾客的护照将由前台工作人员暂时保管,宾客在离船时需将房卡交至前台结账,之后方可取回护照。

Assign rooms to guests and issue room cards. It should be noted that the front desk staff will temporarily keep the guests' passports, guests can retrieve their passports after they hand in their room cards at the front desk for settlement when disembarking.

5.简要向宾客介绍邮轮餐厅的用餐时间、其房间号,以及开船后的救生演习相关说明。

Briefly introduce to guests the dining hours of the cruise restaurant, their room numbers, and the details of the life-saving drill after the ship sails.

6.向宾客提供邮轮服务指南手册,并祝愿宾客旅途愉快。

Provide guests with cruise service guide manuals and wish them a pleasant journey.

7.指引宾客前往邮轮客房。

Direct guests to their cruise cabins.

办理退房的程序(Procedure of Check-out):

1.提前准备好待退房的房号、退房时间、房间内物品的增减情况,以及宾客入住时提出的特殊要求等相关信息。

Prepare information such as the room number of the room to be checked out, the check-out time, the addition or subtraction of items in the room, and the special requests made by the guests during check-in in advance.

2.收到宾客的房卡后,通知客房服务员查房;若宾客要求退房时,应即刻检查房间,重点查看房间物品是否有严重损坏。一旦发现,需与宾客沟通并及时记录相关费用。

After receiving the guest's room card, notify the housekeeping staff to check the room. When the guest requests to check-out, the room should be inspected immediately, with a focus on checking whether there is serious damage to the room items. Once such damage is found, communicate with the guest and record the relevant charges in a timely manner.

3.仔细核对账单,涵盖房费、餐饮费、娱乐费等各项消费,确保无遗漏、无差错后,请宾客签字确认。

Carefully check the bill, covering various expenses such as room charges, catering fees, and entertainment costs. Ensure there are no omissions or errors, and then ask the guest to sign for confirmation.

4.办理结账退房手续,若宾客有消费,从押金中扣除相应金额后将剩余款项退回宾客账户;若宾客无其他消费,则将押金按原支付路径全额退回。

Process the check-out procedure. If the guests have made consumption, deduct the corresponding amount from the deposit and return the remaining balance to the guests' account. If there is no other consumption, return the full deposit via the original payment route.

5.将护照归还给宾客,同时询问宾客是否愿意填写服务满意度调查表,并表达期待下次与宾客相见的美好愿望。

Return the passport to the guests. Meanwhile, ask the guests if they are willing to fill out the service satisfaction survey form and express the anticipation of meeting the guest again.

6.在系统中将房间状态更新为"已退房",并通知客房服务中心。此外,将宾客的账单及相关信息进行存档,以备后续查询与核对。

Update the room status to "checked-out" in the system and notify the Housekeeping Service Center. In addition, file the guest's bill and related information for subsequent inquiries and verifications.

实训任务考核指南
Training Task Assessment Guide

实训任务 Training Task	分值（分） Score（Points）	实际得分 Actual Score
仪容仪表、礼貌礼节 Grooming, Politeness and Etiquette	10	
操作程序 Operating Procedure	20	
操作动作 Operating Action	20	
操作质量 Operating Quality	40	
操作时间 Operating Time	10	
【合计】 Total	100	

任务2 换舱服务
Mission 2
Cabin Reassignment Service

实训目的
Training Objectives

通过实训，学生能够熟悉换舱服务的具体流程，涵盖与宾客沟通、舱房准备、行李转运等环节，掌握换舱服务的操作技巧，进而提高服务质量与效率。

Through hands-on training, students will become familiar with the specific procedures of cabin reassignment service. This includes aspects such as communicating effectively with guests, preparing the cabins, and handling luggage transfer. Master the operation skills of the cabin reassignment service, and then improve the service quality and efficiency.

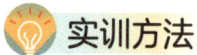

实训方法 Training Method

教师将对换舱服务进行完整示范,详细讲解每一步骤的操作要点与注意事项。示范讲解结束后,学生将分组开展换舱服务的操作训练。在学生操作训练期间,教师将进行巡回指导,留意学生的操作情况,及时给予指导与反馈。为让学生熟练掌握换舱服务的操作技能,需安排学生进行反复强化训练。

The teacher will conduct a complete demonstration of cabin reassignment service, elaborating in detail on the operation key points and precautions for each step. After the demonstration and explanation, students will be divided into groups to carry out hands-on training for cabin reassignment service. During the students' practical training, the teacher will make rounds to guide, pay attention to the students' operation situations, and provide timely guidance and feedback. To enable students to master the operation skills of cabin reassignment service proficiently, it is necessary to arrange for students to conduct repeated intensive training.

实训准备 Training Preparation

行李箱、手推车、接待台桌面、电脑、电话等。

Luggage, trolley, the surface of the reception desk, computer, telephone, etc.

实训内容及操作标准 Training Content and Operating Standards

换舱服务介绍主要涵盖邮轮为宾客提供换舱服务的具体流程。换舱服务通常在宾客提出换房申请时启动,宾客申请换房的原因可能包括个人喜好、舱房设施问题、舱位等级调整或其他因素。具体流程如下:

The introduction to cabin reassignment service mainly covers the specific processes of providing cabin reassignment service to guests on the cruise ship. Cabin reassignment service typically take place when a guest submits a room change request. The reasons for guests to apply for a room change may include personal preferences, problems with cabin facilities, adjustments to cabin class, or other factors. The detailed procedures are as follows:

换舱服务的程序(Procedures for Cabin Reassignment Service):

1.宾客提交换舱申请。宾客可通过邮轮客舱服务电话或前往客服中心提交换舱申请。申请时,宾客需阐明换舱原因,比如对原舱位不满意、期望更换至更高或更低等级舱位、调整舱位想与同伴同舱等。前厅部员工应礼貌记录宾客的姓名、原舱位号、换舱需求及原因。

The guest submits a cabin change request. Guest can submit a cabin change request by calling the cruise ship's cabin service hotline or visiting the guest service center. When applying, they need to clarify the reasons for the change, such as dissatisfaction with the original cabin, the desire to upgrade or downgrade, or the need to adjust the cabin to be with companions. Guest service staff should politely record the guest's name, original cabin number, cabin change requirements, and reasons.

2.前厅部员工评估舱位可调配性。前厅部员工依据邮轮当前舱位的占用状况,评估是否存在能满足宾客需求的空闲舱位。若有可用舱位,前厅部员工需明确舱位的类型、位置、价格等信息。倘若没有合适舱位,前厅部员工应礼貌地向宾客说明情况,并告知后续可能出现的舱位变动信息。

The guest service staff assess the availability of cabins. The guest service staff evaluate whether there are vacant cabins that can meet the guest's needs based on the current occupancy of cabins on the cruise ship. If there are available cabins, the guest service staff need to clarify information such as the type, location, and price of the cabins. If there are no suitable cabins, the guest service staff should politely explain the situation to the guest and inform them of possible future cabin changes.

3.明确新舱位价格。前厅部员工向宾客详细介绍新舱位的相关信息,涵盖价格、位置、设施等方面。宾客根据这些信息,决定是否接受新舱位。若宾客接受新舱位,前厅部员工需告知其换舱所需支付的费用差额(若存在)。

Clarify the price of the new cabin. The guest service staff introduce detailed information about the new cabin to the guest, covering aspects such as price, location, and facilities. The guest decides whether to accept the new cabin based on this information. If the guest accepts the new cabin, the guest service staff need to inform them of the fare difference (if any) required for the cabin change.

4.宾客同意并完成支付。宾客同意换舱后,前厅部员工告知其支付方式和具体支付金额。宾客按照指引完成支付,并留存支付凭证。

The guest agrees and completes the payment. After the guest agrees to the cabin change, the guest service staff inform him of the payment method and the specific payment amount. The guest completes the payment as instructed and keeps the payment receipt.

5.前台办理换舱手续。宾客携带房卡、支付凭证及有效身份证件前往邮轮前台。前台工作人员核对宾客信息,确认支付情况后,办理换舱手续。前台工作人员收回原房卡,并发放新房卡。

The front desk handles the cabin change procedures. The guest goes to the cruise reception desk with the room card, payment receipt, and valid identification. The front desk staff check the guest's information, confirm the payment status, and handle the cabin change procedures. The front desk staff collect the original room card and issue a new one.

6.接收新房卡。宾客领取新房卡后,仔细确认卡上信息准确无误。宾客需妥善保管新房卡,以备后续使用。

Receive the new room card. After receiving the new room card, the guest carefully confirms that the information on the card is correct. The guest should keep the new room card properly for future use.

7.引导至新舱室。前台工作人员或前厅部员工引领宾客前往新舱室。途中,可向宾客介绍邮轮设施和服务,解答宾客疑问。到达新舱室后,协助宾客熟悉环境,确保宾客满意。

Guide to the new cabin. The front desk staff or guest service staff lead the guest to the new cabin. On the way, they can introduce the cruise ship's facilities and services to the guest and answer the guest's questions. After arriving at the new cabin, they assist the guest in getting familiar with the environment to ensure the guest's satisfaction.

8.换舱服务完成确认。宾客确认新舱室设施完好、对环境满意后,在换舱服务确认单上签字。前厅部员工或前台工作人员将确认单存档,作为服务完成的依据。前厅部员工定期回访宾客,了解其对新舱位的满意度,以便持续改进服务质量。

Confirm the completion of the cabin reassignment service. After the guest confirms that the facilities in the new cabin are in good condition and is satisfied with the environment, they sign the cabin reassignment service confirmation form. The guest service staff or front desk staff file the confirmation form as evidence of the completed service. The guest service staff regularly follow up with the guest to understand their satisfaction with the new cabin, so as to continuously improve the service quality.

换舱服务步骤图解
Step Diagram of Cabin Reassignment Service

1.宾客提交换舱申请
The Guest Submits a Cabin Change Request

2.明确新舱位价格
Clarify the Price of the New Cabin

3.宾客同意并完成支付
The Guest Agrees and Completes the Payment

4.接收新房卡
Receive the New Room Card

5.引导至新舱室
Guide to the New Cabin

实训任务考核指南
Training Task Assessment Guide

实训任务 Training Task	分值(分) Score（Points）	实际得分 Actual Score
服务态度 Attitude towards Service	10	
沟通技巧 Communication Skills	20	
应急处理 Emergency Management	20	
专业知识 Professional Knowledge	40	
操作时间 Operating Time	10	
【合计】 Total	100	

任务3 问讯服务
Mission 3 Inquiry Service

实训目的
Training Objectives

本次实训旨在让学生熟练掌握邮轮问讯服务的基本流程、沟通技巧,培养其应对突发情况的能力,从而提高服务质量,满足宾客需求。

This training aims to enable students to master proficiently the basic procedures, communication skills of cruise inquiry service, and the ability to handle unexpected situations in cruise ship inquiry services. As a result, it will improve service quality and meet the needs of guests.

实训方法
Training Method

教师首先介绍问讯服务的重要性以及它在邮轮服务体系中的地位。随后,学生分组开展角色扮演活动,模拟邮轮问讯服务场景。在学生进行操作训练时,教师仔细观察,及时发现问题并给予指导。学生依据教师的指导与反馈,对自身操作方法和技巧做出调整。

The teacher first introduces the importance of inquiry services and their position in the cruise service system. Subsequently, students are divided into groups to carry out role-playing activities, simulating cruise inquiry service scenarios. During the students' operation training, the teacher observes carefully, discovers problems in a timely manner and gives guidance. Students adjust their operation methods and skills according to the teacher's guidance and feedback.

实训准备
Training Preparation

邮轮宣传册、时刻表、地图、宾客留言本、通信设备如电话等。

Cruise brochures, timetables, maps, guest message books, communication equipment such as telephones, etc.

实训内容及操作标准
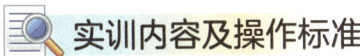
Training Content and Operating Standards

问讯服务是邮轮宾客服务中不可或缺的一环,其目的在于为宾客提供及时、精准且周到的信息服务与指引。借助问讯服务,宾客能够更深入地了解邮轮上的各类设施、活动安排以及服务详情,进而获得更为愉悦、便捷的邮轮旅行体验。具体流程如下:

Inquiry services are an indispensable part of cruise ship guest services. Their purpose is to provide guests with timely, accurate, and considerate information and guidance. Through inquiry services, guests can have a deeper understanding of various facilities, activity arrangements, and service details on the cruise ship, thus obtaining a more pleasant and convenient cruise travel experience. The specific procedures are as follows:

问讯服务的程序(Procedures for Inquiry Services):

1.宾客接待与问候:当宾客抵达问讯处时,服务人员应主动迎上前去,面带微笑、礼貌地打招呼,向宾客表达欢迎之意。同时,确认宾客的身份以及具体需求,为后续服务提供精准信息。

Welcoming and Receiving Guests: when guests arrive at the information desk, service staff should actively step forward, greet them with a warm smile and courtesy, expressing a welcome. At the same time, verify the guests' identities and specific needs to provide accurate information for subsequent services.

2.信息查询与确认:依据宾客提出的需求,细致地查询邮轮的各类信息,涵盖但不限于邮轮设施、活动安排、餐饮服务等方面。务必确认所查询信息的准确性,保证为宾客提供的是最新且可靠的资讯。

Information Inquiry and Verification: according to the needs put forward by guests, carefully search for various information about the cruise ship, covering but not limited to cruise ship facilities, activity arrangements, catering services, etc. It is necessary to confirm the accuracy of the information queried to ensure that the information provided to guests is the latest and reliable.

3.路线指引与说明:根据宾客的目的地,提供详尽的路线指引,包括讲解邮轮内部地图的使用方法。对于路线复杂的区域或者有特殊规定的场所,要给予额外的解释说明,确保宾客能够顺利抵达目的地。

Route Guidance and Explanation: based on the guests' destinations, provide detailed route guidance, including an explanation of how to use the internal map of the cruise ship. For areas with complex routes or special regulations, additional explanations should be given to ensure that guests can reach their destinations smoothly.

4.活动与设施介绍:主动向宾客介绍邮轮上丰富多样的活动以及各类设施,着重突出邮轮的特色服务和亮点项目。结合宾客的兴趣爱好与实际需求,推荐适宜的活动和设施,并告知其预订或参与的具体方式。

Introduction of Activities and Facilities: take the initiative to introduce the rich and diverse activities and various facilities on the cruise ship to guests, especially highlighting the cruise ship's special services and highlight projects. Combine the guests' interests and actual needs, recommend suitable activities and facilities, and inform them of the specific ways to book or participate.

5.特殊需求处理:针对有特殊需求的宾客,比如行动不便、存在语言障碍等情况,要提供个性化服务。积极协调相关部门,切实满足宾客的特殊需求,同时给予必要的协助与支持。

Handling Special Requirements: For guests with special needs, such as those with mobility difficulties or language barriers, personalized services should be provided. Actively coordinate with relevant departments to effectively meet the guests' special needs and provide necessary assistance and support.

6.服务跟进与反馈:在服务过程中,时刻留意宾客需求的变化,及时跟进并灵活调整服务内容。积极鼓励宾客对服务提出反馈意见,以便持续改进和提升服务质量。

Service Follow-up and Feedback: during the service process, always pay attention to the changes in guests' needs, follow up in a timely manner and flexibly adjust the service content. Actively encourage guests to provide feedback on the service to continuously improve and enhance the service quality.

7.记录整理与存档:对每一次问讯服务进行详细记录,内容包括宾客姓名、需求详情、所提供的服务等信息。将记录进行系统整理后妥善存档,便于后续查阅和参考。

Record-keeping and Archiving: make detailed records of each inquiry service, including the guests' names, detailed needs, and the services provided. Systematically organize the records and properly archive them for subsequent reference.

8.服务质量提升:定期深入分析服务记录,总结经验教训,找出服务过程中存在的不足之处以及可改进的要点。依据分析结果制定针对性的改进措施,并定期对服务人员开展培训与指导工作,以此提升整体服务质量。

Service Auality Enhancement: regularly conduct in-depth analysis of service records, summarize experiences and lessons, identify the short comings and improvement points in the service process. According to the analysis results, formulate targeted improvement measures and regularly conduct training and guidance for service staff to improve the overall service quality.

实训任务考核指南
Training Task Assessment Guide

实训任务 Training Task	分值（分） Score (Points)	实际得分 Actual Score
礼仪态度 Politeness and Demeanor	10	
信息准确性 Precision of Information	20	
表达能力 Communicative Abilities	20	
专业知识 Professional Knowledge	40	
解决问题能力 Problem-solving Capabilities	10	
【合计】 Total	100	

任务 4　总机服务
Mission 4　Operator Service

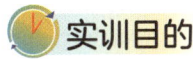 **实训目的**
Learning Objectives

　　本次实训旨在让学生熟练掌握邮轮总机服务的各项操作技能，涵盖接听电话、转接电话、提供咨询服务等方面，从而实现提高服务质量、满足宾客需求的目标。

This training aims at equipping students with the necessary operational skills for cruise operator services, such as call handling, call transferring, and providing consultations, in order to enhance service quality and meet guest expectations.

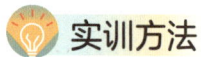
实训方法
Training Method

教师详细讲解总机服务的基本操作流程、技能要求及注意事项,并现场演示接听电话、转接电话等关键步骤。在教师讲解与示范后,学生分组展开实际操作训练。在学生操作训练期间,教师全程指导,及时纠正学生的错误操作,同时给予积极的反馈与建议。

The teacher will comprehensively explain the basic operational procedures, requisite skills, and matters needing attention for operator service. Additionally, the teacher will demonstrate critical tasks such as call answering and call transferring on-site. Following the teacher's explanation and demonstration, students will be organized into groups to engage in practical hands-on training. Throughout this training, the teacher will offer continuous supervision, promptly correcting any erroneous actions by students while providing constructive feedback and recommendations.

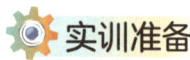
实训准备
Training Preparation

电话交换机、话务台、耳机、麦克风等。

Telephone exchange, telephone operator console, headset, microphone, etc.

实训内容及操作标准
Training Content and Operating Standards

总机接线员是邮轮上的重要接待人员,主要负责接听并处理船上的所有来电,为宾客提供高效、准确且友好的电话服务。他们需要具备良好的沟通技巧、应变能力,同时掌握丰富的邮轮业务知识,以此确保宾客的需求能够得到及时满足。具体程序如下:

The ship's telephone operators are important reception personnel on the cruise ship. They are mainly responsible for answering and handling all incoming calls on board and providing guests with efficient, accurate and friendly telephone services. They need to possess excellent communication skills, strong adaptability, and a wealth of knowledge about cruise business, so as to ensure that guests' needs can be met in a timely manner. The specific procedures are as follows:

总机服务的程序(Procedures for Operator Services):

1.接听电话:总机接线员应在电话铃响三声内接听电话,保持语气亲切、礼貌。使用标准问候语,如:"您好,邮轮总机,请问有什么可以帮到您?"

Answering Calls: the ship's telephone operator is expected to answer incoming calls promptly, within three rings, while maintaining a polite and friendly tone. Standard greetings such as "Good day, ship's operator. How may I assist you?" should be used.

2.了解宾客需求:仔细聆听宾客的询问或需求,在提供相应的服务信息或转接电话之前确保准确理解宾客需求。

Understanding Guest Needs: carefully listen to the inquiries or needs of guests and ensure a comprehensive understanding before providing relevant service information or transferring the call.

3.转接电话:如宾客需要转接至邮轮内部其他部门,总机接线员应迅速、准确地完成转接。转接前,应确认对方部门是否在线,避免转接失败。

Call Transfer: if a guest requires a call transfer to another department within the ship, the ship's telephone operator should carry out the transfer promptly and accurately after confirming that the receiving department is available to avoid unsuccessful transfers.

4.提供信息咨询:如宾客询问关于邮轮设施、服务、活动等方面的信息,总机接线员应准确、全面地回答。对于不熟悉的问题,接线员可查询相关资料或请教同事后再回答。

Providing Information Consultation: when guests inquire about ship facilities, services, or activities, it is essential for the ship's telephone operator to offer accurate and detailed responses. For unfamiliar queries, consulting relevant resources or colleagues before responding is advisable.

5.处理紧急情况:如遇宾客报告紧急情况,总机接线员应保持冷静,迅速记录并通知相关部门处理。根据情况,提供必要的指导和安抚,确保宾客安全。

Managing Emergencies: in case of an emergency reported by a guest, it is crucial for the ship's telephone operator to remain composed while swiftly documenting the details and notifying relevant departments for immediate action. Offering necessary guidance and reassurance based on the situation, ensures guest safety.

6.结束通话:通话结束前,总机接线员应使用礼貌用语,如:"祝您生活愉快,再见!"等待宾客挂断电话后,才轻轻放下话筒。

Ending Calls: before concluding a conversation with a polite phrase like "Have an enjoyable day; goodbye," the ship's telephone operator should wait for guests to disconnect first before gently replacing the receiver.

总机服务步骤图解
Step Diagram of Operator Service

1.礼貌接听电话

Answer the Phone in a Courteous Manner

2.记录宾客需求

Document the Requirements of the Guests

3.转接电话
Call Transfer

4.轻放结束通话
Conclude the Call with a Gentle Disconnection

实训任务考核指南
Training Task Assessment Guide

实训任务 Training Task	分值(分) Score (Points)	实际得分 Actual Score
沟通表达 Communicating and Expressing	10	
服务态度 Attitude towards Service	20	
操作流程 Procedures for Operation	30	
专业知识 Professional Knowledge	40	
【合计】 Total	100	

任务 5　收银服务
Mission 5
Cashier Service

实训目的
Learning Objectives

教师讲解邮轮收银服务的操作程序和要求,学生进行邮轮收银服务操作技能的训练。借此,学生能够了解并掌握邮轮收银服务的操作程序、标准与要领,达成熟知操作程序与规范的训练要求。

Through the teacher's explanation of the operation procedures and requirements of cruise cashier service and the students' training in operation skills, students can understand and master the operation procedures, standards and essentials of cruise cashier service, and meet the training requirements of being familiar with the operation procedures and standards.

实训方法
Training Method

首先,由教师进行示范讲解,随后学生展开动手操作训练。在学生操作训练期间,教师实时予以指导,学生通过反复强化练习,从而达到熟练掌握该项操作技能的目的。

Firstly, the teacher conducts a demonstration and gives an explanation. Subsequently, the students start hands-on operation training. During the students' operation training period, the teacher provides real-time guidance. The students achieve the goal of mastering the operation skills through repeated intensive practice.

实训准备
Training Preparation

前台接待台、电脑、若干练功券、房卡、验钞机、押金单、计算器、滚珠笔等。

Reception desk, computer, several banknote-training vouchers, room card, counterfeit money detector/note detector, deposit receipt, calculator, rollerball pen, etc.

实训内容及操作标准
Training Content and Operating Standards

作为一名合格的邮轮前台收银员,不仅要具备扎实的前台收银服务理论知识,更重要的是要熟练掌握前台收银技能。而这些技能主要通过实际操作来展现,具体程序如下:

As a qualified cruise reception desk cashier, not only should one possess solid theoretical knowledge of front desk cashier services, but more importantly, one should master front desk cashier skills proficiently. These skills are mainly demonstrated through practical operations. The specific procedures are as follows:

收银服务的程序(以预存现金为例)[Procedure of Cashier Service (A Example of Cash Deposit)]:

1.主动向宾客致以问候,礼貌询问宾客需要何种帮助。
Take the initiative to greet guests and politely inquire about the assistance they require.

2.请宾客出示其在邮轮上领取的房卡。
Please ask the guests to present the room card they received on the cruise.

3.根据邮轮相关规定,明确告知宾客需缴纳的货币种类以及现金金额。
Inform guests of the type of currency and the amount of cash required according to the cruise regulations.

4.礼貌询问宾客的支付方式。
Politely ask the guests about their preferred payment method.

5.在宾客面前仔细清点现金数量,并通过验钞机查验货币真伪。
Count the cash carefully in front of the guests and verify the authenticity of the currency with a currency detector.

6.开具押金单,同时请宾客在单据上签名予以确认。
Issue a deposit receipt, and ask guests to sign the receipt for confirmation

7.协助宾客开通在船上的消费账户以及房卡刷卡签账功能。
Assist guests in opening their onboard consumption accounts and enabling the room card's charge-signing function.

8.告知宾客办理手续已全部完成,并预祝宾客拥有一段愉快的旅程。
Inform the guests that the formalities have been fully completed and wish them a pleasant journey.

收银服务步骤图解
Step Diagram of Cashier Service

1.问候
Greeting

2.提供房卡
Offer Room Card

3.告知通用货币种类
Inform the Type of Common Currency

4.清点现金
Count Cash

5.签押金单
Sign a Deposit Receipt

6.办理完成
Complete the Process

实训任务考核指南
Training Task Assessment Guide

实训任务 Training Task	分值(分) Score (Points)	实际得分 Actual Score
仪容仪表、礼貌礼节 Grooming, Politeness and Etiquette	10	
操作程序 Operating Procedure	20	
操作动作 Operating Action	20	
操作质量 Operating Quality	40	
操作时间 Operating Time	10	
【合计】 Total	100	

收银服务的程序(以信用卡关联为例)[Procedure of Cashier Service (A Example of Credit Card)]

1.主动热情地向宾客致以问候,礼貌询问宾客需要提供何种帮助。

Take the initiative to greet guests and politely inquire about the assistance they require.

2.礼貌地请宾客出示其在邮轮上领取的房卡。

Politely ask the guests to present the room card they received on the cruise.

3.依据邮轮的相关规定,清晰明确地告知宾客需要缴纳的货币种类以及预授权金额。

Inform guests of the type of currency and pre-authorization amount required according to the cruise regulations.

4.以礼貌的方式询问宾客的支付方式。

Politely ask the guests about their preferred payment method.

5.在POS机上进行操作,协助宾客完成预授权刷取。

Operate the POS machine to assist guests in completing the pre-authorization process.

6.POS机自动打印出预授权单,将商户存根联递给宾客,请宾客签字确认。

The POS machine will automatically print out the pre-authorization form. Hand the merchant's copy to the guests for signature and confirmation.

7.协助宾客开通在船上的消费账户以及房卡刷卡签账功能。

Assist guests in opening their onboard consumption accounts and enabling the room card's charge-signing function.

模块4 前台接待服务
Module 4 Reception Service

8.告知宾客办理手续已全部完成,并衷心预祝宾客拥有一段愉快的旅程。
Inform the guests that all formalities have been completed and sincerely wish them a pleasant journey.

实训任务考核指南
Training Task Assessment Guide

实训任务 Training Task	分值(分) Score(Points)	实际得分 Actual Score
仪容仪表、礼貌礼节 Grooming, Politeness and Etiquette	10	
操作程序 Operating Procedure	20	
操作动作 Operating Action	20	
操作质量 Operating Quality	40	
操作时间 Operating Time	10	
【合计】 Total	100	

任务6 客诉处理
Mission 6 Guest Complaint

实训目的
Training Objectives

教师讲解邮轮客诉服务的操作程序和要求,学生进行邮轮客诉服务操作技能的训练。借此,学生能够了解并掌握邮轮客诉服务的操作程序、标准与要领,达成熟知操作程序与规范的训练要求。

Through the teacher's explanation of the operation procedures and requirements of cruise guest complaint service and the students' training in operation skills, students can understand

and master the operation procedures, standards and essentials of cruise guest complaint service, and meet the training requirements of being familiar with the operation procedures and standards.

实训方法 Training Method

首先,由教师进行示范讲解,随后学生展开动手操作训练。在学生操作训练期间,教师予以实时指导,学生通过反复强化练习,从而达到熟练掌握该项操作技能的目的。

Firstly, the teacher conducts a demonstration and gives an explanation. Subsequently, the students start hands-on operation training. During the students' operation training period, the teacher provides real-time guidance. The students achieve the goal of mastering the operation skills through repeated intensive practice.

实训准备 Training Preparation

前台接待台、电脑、电话机、客诉记录本、房卡、滚珠笔等。

Reception desk, computer, telephone, guest complaint book, room card, rollerball pen, etc.

实训内容及操作标准 Training Content and Operating Standards

作为一名合格的邮轮前台接待员,不仅要具备扎实的前台接待理论知识,更为关键的是要熟练掌握处理前台客诉的操作技能。这些技能主要通过实际操作得以展现。具体程序如下:

As a qualified cruise reception desk receptionist, one should not only possess solid theoretical knowledge of front desk reception, but more importantly, should master the operation skills of handling front desk guest complaints proficiently. These skills are mainly demonstrated through practical operations. The specific procedures are as follows:

客诉处理的程序(Procedures for Handling Guest Complaints):

1.提前做好心理准备,迎接前来投诉的宾客。

Prepare mentally in advance to receive guests who come to complain.

2.接待投诉宾客时,即刻向宾客致歉,并邀请宾客到沙发处就座稍做休息。

When receiving a complaining guest, immediately apologize to the guest and invite the guest to take a seat on the sofa and have a short rest.

3.耐心倾听宾客的每一句话,让宾客充分宣泄情绪,同时认真做好记录。

Listen patiently to every word the guest says, allow the guest to fully vent emotions, and carefully take notes at the same time.

4.向宾客展现同理心,使宾客从单纯投诉转变为愿意倾诉。

Show empathy to the guest, so that the guest changes from simply complaining to being willing to talk.

5.剖析宾客的真正需求,在自身授权范围内探寻最佳解决方案。

Analyze the guest's real needs and explore the best solution within one's own authorized scope.

6.对宾客的理解表示感谢。

Express gratitude for the guest's understanding.

7.确保对宾客承诺的事项得到跟进与落实。

Ensure that the matters promised to the guest are followed up and implemented.

8.倘若遇到难以处理的状况,立即向上级寻求协助。

If encountering a difficult-to-handle situation, immediately seek assistance from superiors.

9.详细记录事件的起因、经过、处理方案以及最终结果等内容。

Record in detail the cause, process, treatment plan, final result and other content of the incident.

客诉处理步骤图解
Step Diagram of Guest Complaint

1.做好接待准备

Get Ready for Reception

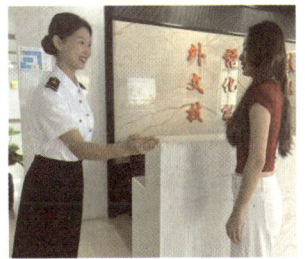

2.请客人入坐沙发

Take a Seat on the Sofa

3.耐心倾听并记录

Listen Patiently and Take Notes

4.最好的解决方案

The Best Solution

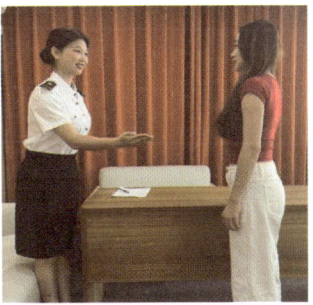

5.感谢宾客

Thank the Guest

6.汇报记录

Report Record

实训任务考核指南

Training Task Assessment Guide

实训任务 Training Task	分值(分) Score (Points)	实际得分 Actual Score
仪容仪表、礼貌礼节 Grooming, Politeness and Etiquette	10	
操作程序 Operating Procedure	20	
操作动作 Operating Action	20	
操作质量 Operating Quality	40	
操作时间 Operating Time	10	
【合计】 Total	100	

项目 2 前台接待服务常见问题处理
Project 2 Handling the Common Problem of Reception Service

任务 1 常见案例分享
Mission 1 Common Case Sharing

案例 1 更换舱房（Case 1 Change Cabin）

在邮轮前台接待工作中,宾客提出更换舱房的需求颇为常见。2023 年 9 月 15 日,李女士预订了一趟邮轮行程,航期为 10 月 1 日至 10 月 7 日。登船后,依照舱房服务员的引导,李女士顺利找到了自己的房间。然而,当她将房卡插入电槽时,电灯毫无反应,致使房间光线昏暗。李女士当即走出船舱,向前台接待员说明情况。前台接待员得知后,先对李女士进行安抚,随即通知舱房服务员前往处理。经检查,发现整个房间的电路均无法正常运作,舱房服务员遂将情况反馈至邮轮前台。前台接待员了解详情后,立刻为李女士更换了同类型的房间,向她表达了诚挚歉意,并安排赠送欢迎水果,以表歉意与关怀。

One of the most common situations that cruise reception desk receptionists encounter is guests' requests for cabin changes. On September 15, 2023, Ms. Li booked a cruise with a sailing period from October 1st to October 7th. After boarding the ship, following the guidance of the cabin attendant, Ms. Li located her room. When she inserted the room card into the electrical slot, the light did not come on, leaving the room dimly lit. Ms. Li immediately left her cabin to report the situation to the front desk staff. Upon learning of the issue, the front desk staff first soothed Ms. Li and then promptly informed the cabin attendant to handle it. After inspection, it was found that the entire room's electrical system was malfunctioning.

The cabin attendant then reported the situation back to the front desk. After learning the details, the front desk staff immediately arranged for Ms. Li to be moved to a similar-type cabin. They expressed sincere apologies and arranged to send welcome fruit as a gesture of apology and care.

案例 2　升舱服务（Case 2 Cabin Upgrade Service）

邮轮公司会依据会员需求，提供更具价值的服务，例如为 VIP 宾客升级房间。张女士是某邮轮公司的忠实顾客，此前已登船游玩十几次。此次，张女士携朋友再度登上这艘邮轮。前台接待员查看张女士的客史信息后，考虑到邮轮上高价位客舱尚有几间空余，便即刻申请为张女士免费升舱。张女士登船后得知自己获得免费升舱，十分高兴，在微信朋友圈大力宣传该邮轮公司的优质服务。

Cruise lines will provide more valuable services according to the needs of their members. For example, they will upgrade the cabins for VIP guests. Ms. Zhang is a loyal customer of a certain cruise company and has boarded the ship for more than a dozen times. This time, Ms. Zhang, along with her friends, came aboard this cruise again. After checking Ms. Zhang's guest history information, the front desk receptionist, considering that there were still several high-priced cabins available on the cruise, immediately applied for a free cabin upgrade for Ms. Zhang. When Ms. Zhang boarded the ship and learned that she had received a free upgrade, she was extremely happy and vigorously promoted the excellent services of this cruise company in her WeChat Moments.

案例 3　宾客物品丢失（Case 3 Guest Items Lost）

刘女士乘坐邮轮出游，早上起床后发现自己的手提包不见了。她在客舱内四处寻找，却一无所获。于是，刘女士致电前台接待员寻求帮助。前台接待员接到刘女士的电话后，首先安抚了她的情绪，并承诺会竭尽全力帮她寻找手提包。接着，接待员让刘女士回忆昨晚去过哪些地方。刘女士回忆道，昨晚去餐厅用餐时手提包还在，之后去剧场观看了表演，结束后便直接回舱房休息了。前台接待员随即帮刘女士向餐厅询问昨晚是否有遗留物品。果不其然，刘女士昨晚将手提包遗落在了餐厅，目前手提包在餐厅的失物招领处。前台接待员立即通知刘女士携带本人身份证件前往餐厅领取手提包。

Ms. Liu took a cruise for a trip. When she woke up in the morning, she found that her handbag was missing. She searched everywhere in the cabin but found nothing. So she called the front desk receptionist for help. After answering Ms. Liu's call, the front desk receptionist first soothed her emotions and promised to do everything possible to help her find the handbag. Then, the receptionist asked Ms. Liu to recall where she had been the previous night. Ms. Liu recalled that she had the handbag with her when she went to the restaurant for dinner last night. After that, she went to the theater to watch a performance and then went straight back to the cabin to rest. The front desk receptionist immediately inquired with the restaurant on behalf of Ms. Liu whether there were any lost items left there last night. Sure enough, Ms. Liu had left her handbag in the restaurant last night and it was currently at the lost-and-found office of the restaurant. The front desk receptionist immediately informed Ms. Liu to bring her identification documents and go to the restaurant to claim her handbag.

案例4　更换船卡（Case 4 Replacement of Ship Card）

邮轮上,宾客的船卡极为重要。船卡不仅是宾客身份的标识,更是挂账消费的凭证。黄女士在邮轮游玩期间,不慎将船卡遗失,便前往前台,请求接待员为其补发一张船卡。接待员详细询问事情经过后,先是协助黄女士寻找船卡,而后为其注销了丢失的船卡,并制作了一张新船卡交给黄女士。同时,接待员温馨提醒黄女士,船卡丢失需按规定赔偿相应费用,请务必妥善保管。若再次不慎丢失,可随时前往前台办理注销及补办手续。此外,接待员还特别叮嘱,船卡应避免与手机、相机、电视机等易产生磁场的物品放置在一起,否则极易导致船卡消磁。一旦船卡消磁,同样可到前台进行加磁处理。

The ship card of guests on the cruise is of great importance. It is not only an identification of guests' identity but also a voucher for charge-on-account consumption. Ms. Huang accidentally lost her ship card during her cruise trip. So she went to the front desk and asked the receptionist to issue her a new one. After the receptionist inquired about the details, she first assisted Ms. Huang in looking for the ship card. Then she cancelled the lost ship card and made a new one for Ms. Huang. Meanwhile, the receptionist kindly reminded Ms. Huang that there would be a corresponding charge for a lost ship card and she should keep it carefully. If she lost it again, she could come to the front desk at any time to cancel the old one and get a replacement. In addition, the receptionist especially reminded that the ship card should be kept away from items that can generate magnetic fields, such as mobile phones, cameras, and televisions, as it could easily get demagnetized. Once it was demagnetized, she could also come to the front desk to have it remagnetized.

案例5　邮轮随意更换舱房(Case 5 Cruise Ships Change Cabins at Will)

所有邮轮公司均禁止宾客私自更换舱房,这是因为私自更换舱房会干扰电脑记账的准确性,同时影响行李的正常派送。若宾客有更换舱房的需求,应当前往邮轮前台办理相关手续。邮轮前台接待员会根据可更换舱房的实际数量进行考量,只有在条件允许的情况下,才会同意为宾客正式更换舱房。倘若更换舱房涉及差价补缴,宾客需及时补足差价。

All cruise lines prohibit guests from changing cabins on their own. This is because unauthorized cabin changes can interfere with the accuracy of computerized bookkeeping and disrupt the proper delivery of luggage. If guests wish to change their cabins, they should go to the cruise reception desk to complete the relevant formalities. The receptionist will take into account the actual number of available cabins for replacement and will only agree to officially change the cabin when conditions permit. If a price difference needs to be paid for the cabin change, guests are required to pay up the difference in a timely manner.

案例 6　宾客中途离船（Case 6 Guest Disembarks Midway）

在正常情况下，邮轮公司不允许宾客中途离船。若宾客因特殊原因确需中途离船，由此产生的所有费用均需宾客自行承担，并且邮轮上已收取的相关费用一律不予退还。

Under normal circumstances, cruise companies do not allow guests to disembark from the ship midway. If guests have special reasons to disembark midway, all the costs incurred shall be borne by the guests themselves, and the relevant fees already charged by the cruise line will not be refunded under any circumstances.

案例 7　宾客行李遗失（Case 7 Lost Guest Luggage）

李女士进入舱房后，向邮轮前台接待员反映，同行朋友的行李都已送达房间，可自己的行李却不见踪影，怀疑行李遗失了。前台接待员接到李女士的反馈后，仔细询问了其行李的特征，随后立即与相关部门取得联系，并跟进后续工作。一旦收到相关部门的任何反馈，接待员承诺会第一时间将情况告知李女士。

After entering the cabin, Ms. Li reported to the cruise reception desk receptionist that her friends' luggage had all been delivered to the room, but her own luggage was nowhere to be seen. She suspected that her luggage was lost. After receiving Ms. Li's report, the receptionist carefully inquired about the characteristics of her luggage. Then, the receptionist immediately got in touch with the relevant departments and followed up on the subsequent work. Once any feedback was received from the relevant departments, the receptionist promised to inform Ms. Li of the situation immediately.

案例 8　宾客要求邮轮前台协助办理签证（Case 8 Guest Requests the Cruise Reception Desk to Help Him with Visa Application）

李女士在登船前未办妥日本和韩国的签证，上船之后却萌生出前往这两个国家的岸上参观的想法，于是她向邮轮前台提出了协助办理签证的诉求。

Ms. Li hadn't obtained the visas for Japan and R.O.Korea before boarding the cruise. After getting on board, she developed the idea of visiting the shores of these two countries, so she asked the cruise reception desk for assistance in visa processing.

前台接待员在接到李女士的请求后，一时无法当场给出确切答复，便礼貌地请李女士稍做等候，随即向部门经理进行咨询。在详细了解相关政策和邮轮公司的服务权限后，接待员回到前台，向李女士耐心解释道："非常理解您想去岸上参观的心情，不过很抱歉，邮轮前台无法直接为您办理日、韩两国的签证。但我们会全力协助您收集和整理办理签证所需的资料，在邮轮靠岸后，及时将这些资料提交给相关部门。"

Upon receiving Ms. Li's request, the receptionist couldn't give an immediate definite answer. Politely, the receptionist asked Ms. Li to wait for a while and then consulted the department manager. After thoroughly understanding the relevant policies and the service scope of the cruise company, the receptionist returned to the front desk and patiently explained to Ms. Li, "We fully understand your eagerness to visit the shore. However, we're sorry to inform you that the cruise front desk can't directly process the visas for Japan and South Korea. But we will do our best to assist you in gathering and organizing the materials required for visa application. Once the cruise ship docks, we will promptly submit these materials to the relevant authorities."

接着,接待员告知李女士办理日、韩签证可能需要准备的基础材料:"办理日本签证,通常需要您准备有效期在6个月以上的护照原件、身份证正反面复印件、户口本整本复印件、近期白色背景的彩色照片,以及能证明您经济能力的材料,像银行存款证明、信用卡账单、在职证明等。而办理韩国签证,所需材料也大致类似,比如护照原件、白底彩照、身份证及户口本复印件。如果您是在职人员,还需要提供在职证明;若您能提供资产证明,如房产、车产证明或银行流水明细等,会对签证申请更有帮助。此外,如果您符合特定条件,例如本科以上及毕业3年内的学生,办理签证所需的材料会有所简化。"

Subsequently, the receptionist informed Ms. Li about the basic materials usually needed for Japanese and R.O. Korea visa applications. "For a Japanese visa, you generally need to prepare the original passport with a validity period of more than six months, copies of both sides of your ID card, a copy of the entire household register, recent color photos with a white background, and materials to prove your financial capacity, such as bank deposit certificates, credit card statements, and an employment certificate, etc. The materials required for a South Korean visa are roughly similar, such as the original passport, color photos with a white background, copies of your ID card and household register. If you are employed, you also need to provide an employment certificate. Additionally, if you can provide asset certificates, like property deeds, vehicle ownership certificates, or bank statement details, it will be more conducive to your visa application. Moreover, if you meet certain specific conditions, for example, if you are an undergraduate or have graduated within the past three years, the materials required for visa application will be simplified."

最后,接待员温馨提醒李女士:"由于办理签证所需时间和具体要求可能因个人情况和政策变动而有所不同,建议您密切关注我们的通知,及时补充可能需要的额外材料,以便我们能更顺利地协助您完成签证申请流程。"

Finally, the receptionist kindly reminded Ms. Li, "Since the time required for visa processing and the specific requirements may vary depending on individual circumstances and policy changes, we suggest that you pay close attention to our notifications and promptly provide any additional materials that may be needed, so that we can assist you in smoothly completing the visa application process."

案例9 宾客带领婴儿上船,并且不占床位(Case 9 a Guest Takes a Baby on Board and Does Not Occupy a Bed)

张女士一家四口预订了一个三人位的舱房。在办理入住手续时,邮轮前台接待员告知张女士,按照规定,每个人都需要购买一个床位,即便是婴儿也不例外。对此,张女士感到十分不解。

Ms. Zhang's family of four booked a three-berth cabin. When going through the check-in procedures, the cruise reception desk receptionist informed Ms. Zhang that according to the regulations, everyone, even the baby, needed to purchase a berth. Ms. Zhang was quite puzzled by this.

需要说明的是,邮轮运营受《国际海上人命安全公约》的严格管制。该公约明确规定,为避免超载情况的发生,每位宾客,无论是成人、儿童还是婴儿,都必须单独占用一个床位。因此,像张女士这样一家四口的情况,必须要预订和购买拥有四个床位的舱房。

It should be noted that the operation of cruise ships is strictly regulated by the International Convention for the Safety of Life at Sea. This convention clearly stipulates that to prevent overloading, every guest, whether an adult, a child, or an infant, must occupy a separate berth. Therefore, for a family of four like Ms. Zhang's, they must book and purchase a cabin with four berths.

案例 10 宾客需要提供婴儿用品（Case 10 Visitors Need to Provide Baby Supplies）

邮轮上的婴儿用品数量有限。若此前已有众多宾客申请使用,后续宾客可能就无法获得足够的婴儿用品。因此,在宾客预订时,就应提示其是否需要婴儿用品,以避免出现供应不足的情况。

The number of baby products on the cruise ship is limited. If a large number of previous guests have applied for their use, subsequent guests may not be able to obtain sufficient baby products. Therefore, when guests make a reservation, they should be reminded to indicate whether they need baby products, so as to avoid a situation of insufficient supply.

案例 11 宾客私下互换房卡（Case 11 Guests Exchange Room Cards Privately）

李女士一行共预订了三间舱房。晚上,李女士想和隔壁房间的张女士彻夜长谈,于是便与张女士同住者交换了房卡使用。然而,邮轮上明确禁止私自交换房卡的行为。这是因为房卡在邮轮上有着非常重要的作用,它不仅是开启房间的钥匙,还是宾客在船上进行消费记账的凭证,同时也是办理通关手续时领取上岸许可证的关键凭证。倘若私下交换房卡,极有可能引发记账错误,进而对宾客下船时的结算造成不利影响。邮轮前台接待员得知李女士的这一行为后,立刻告知她这种做法是不被允许的,并建议李女士若有需求,可以前往前台办理换舱房手续。

Ms. Li and her group booked three cabins in total. At night, Ms. Li desired to have an all-night chat with Ms. Zhang in the adjacent room. Thus, she swapped her room card with that of Ms. Zhang's roommate. However, on the cruise ship, the unauthorized exchange of room cards is strictly prohibited. This is because the room card serves multiple crucial functions. Not only is it the key to the room, but it is also the accounting voucher for guests' onboard expenses and the essential document for obtaining the shore-landing permit when going through customs formalities on the cruise. If room cards are privately exchanged, there is a high likelihood of causing accounting errors, which will have an adverse impact on guests' settlement when disembarking. Once the cruise reception desk receptionist learned of Ms. Li's action, he/she immediately informed her that such behavior was not permitted and suggested that if she had the need, she could go to the front desk to handle the cabin-changing procedures.

案例 12　为宾客打造个性化服务（Case 12 Creating Personalized Services for Visitors）

史密斯夫妇在前台出示护照办理入住手续时，前台接待员发现入住当天正是史密斯夫人的生日，同时还得知当天也是他们夫妻结婚 25 周年的银婚纪念日。前台接待员随即将这一情况通知了客舱服务员，让其对宾客的房间进行精心布置：用客房毛巾叠出栩栩如生的动物造型，并在房间内撒上玫瑰花瓣；又通知餐饮服务员准备一份精美的生日蛋糕，悄悄放入房间，给夫妇俩一个惊喜。史密斯夫妇入住后惊喜不已，对邮轮提供的贴心服务十分满意。在行程结束离开时，他们特意给前台工作人员写了一封表扬信，以表达诚挚的谢意。

When Mr. and Mrs. Smith presented their passports to check-in at the front desk, the staff discovered that it was Mrs. Smith's birthday and also learned that it was the couple's 25th-anniversary silver wedding day. The front desk staff immediately informed the cabin crew to carefully decorate the guests' room. The crew was instructed to fold lifelike animals with the guest room towels and scatter rose petals in the room. Additionally, the front desk staff notified the catering crew to prepare an exquisite birthday cake and quietly place it in the room to surprise the couple. After checking in, Mr. and Mrs. Smith were extremely delighted and highly satisfied with the thoughtful service provided by the cruise. At the end of their trip when they were about to leave, they specifically wrote a letter of commendation to the front desk staff to express their sincere gratitude.

案例 13　宾客付费升舱，增加客房销售额（Case 13 Guests Pay for Upgrades to Increase Room Sales）

李女士带着一家五口在邮轮前台办理入住手续时，前台接待员注意到李女士带着一对十分可爱的双胞胎。恰逢此次邮轮航线上的亲子套房尚有空闲，为提升宾客体验并增加部门销售额，前台接待员向李女士介绍了配备亲子玩具、亲子帐篷以及各类亲子设施设备的亲子智能套房，同时给予了升房差价折扣。李女士欣然接受，支付差价进行了升级，并愉快地带着一家人入住了亲子智能套房。

When Ms. Li and her family of five checked in at the cruise reception desk, the cruise reception desk staff noticed that Ms. Li had a pair of extremely cute twins. Coincidentally, there were still some vacancies in the parent-child suites on this cruise route. To enhance the guests' experience and boost the department's sales, the front desk staff introduced to Ms. Li the parent-child smart suite, which was equipped with parent-child toys, parent-child tents, and various parent-child facilities and equipment. Meanwhile, they offered her a discount on the room upgrade price difference. Ms. Li readily accepted the offer, paid the price difference for the upgrade, and happily checked in with her family to the parent-child smart suite.

案例 14 主动迎接宾客（Case 14 Proactively Greet Guests）

张先生带着年迈的父母登船办理入住手续时，前台接待员见状，立刻主动将他们引领至靠近前台的休息区域就座，随后在该休息区域协助他们办理入住手续，以免两位老人因长时间站立而身体不适。

When Mr. Zhang boarded the ship with his elderly parents to check-in, the front desk staff, noticing their situation, immediately and proactively led them to the rest area near the front desk. Subsequently, the staff assisted them in handling the check-in procedures right in that rest area, so as to prevent the two elderly people from feeling unwell due to standing for an extended period.

案例 15 及时主动为宾客答疑解惑（Case 15 Take the Initiative to Answer Questions for Guests in a Timely Manner）

来自德国的米勒夫妇首次乘坐邮轮出行。前台接待员在为他们办理入住手续时了解到这一情况后，用流利的英语主动向米勒夫妇介绍了邮轮餐厅的用餐时间、地点，以及主要游玩设施设备的情况。接待员还递给米勒夫妇一本英文的邮轮服务项目指南，该指南详细介绍了邮轮上的娱乐项目，以便他们能更好地享受邮轮服务。米勒夫妇对此表示衷心感谢。离船后，他们在自己的社交媒体上分享了邮轮游玩经历，并极力推荐这艘邮轮。

It was the first time that Mr. and Mrs. Miller from Germany had taken a cruise. When the front desk staff learned about this while handling their check-in procedures, they proactively introduced, in fluent English, the dining hours, locations of the cruise ship's restaurants, and the main recreational facilities and equipment to Mr. and Mrs. Miller. Additionally, the staff handed them an English-language cruise service guide, which detailed the cruise's entertainment programs, enabling the couple to better enjoy the cruise services. The Millers expressed their sincere gratitude. After disembarking, they shared their cruise-going experiences on their social media and highly recommended this cruise ship.

模块 5
岸上观光服务
Module 5
Shore Excursion Service

认识岸上观光服务 项目 1

Know about Shore Excursion Service / Project 1

任务 1　岸上观光部门职责

Mission 1
Duty of Shore Excursion Department

实训目的
Training Objectives

通过教师对邮轮岸上观光部门职责的介绍,学生能够了解岸上观光部的工作内容与要求,掌握为宾客提供岸上观光服务的操作要领,达成熟知操作程序与规范的训练目标。

Through the teacher's introduction to the responsibilities of the cruise ship's shore excursion department, students are able to understand the work content and requirements of the shore excursion department. They can acquire and master the operational essentials of providing shore excursion services to guests, thereby attaining the training objective of being well-versed in the operational procedures and specifications.

实训方法
Training Method

首先,教师进行示范讲解,随后学生展开动手操作训练。在学生操作训练期间,教师加以指导,学生反复强化训练,以此达成熟练掌握该项操作技能的目标。

Firstly, the teacher gives a demonstration and offers an explanation. Subsequently, the students carry out hands-on operation training. During the students' operation training, the teacher provides guidance, and the students conduct repeated intensive training to achieve the goal of mastering this operational skill proficiently.

实训准备
Training Preparation

白板、白板笔、分组讨论任务单、实训手册等。

Whiteboard, whiteboard markers, group discussion task sheets, practical training manuals, etc.

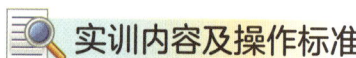
实训内容及操作标准
Training Content and Operating Standards

作为一名合格的邮轮前厅服务员,需要具备扎实的前厅服务理论知识。岸上观光是邮轮旅游的重要组成部分,宾客在邮轮靠港时会积极参与陆地观光行程,因此岸上观光部门的工作人员需要提前为宾客做好规划安排。豪华邮轮旅游需要搭配适宜的陆地观光线路,如此才能为宾客打造完美的旅行体验。

As a qualified cruise front desk attendant, one needs to possess solid theoretical knowledge of front desk services. Shore excursions are an essential part of cruise tourism. When the cruise ship docks, guests actively participate in land-based sightseeing itineraries. Therefore, the staff of the shore-excursion department need to make advance plans and arrangements for the guests. Luxury cruise tourism requires suitable land-based sightseeing itineraries to create a perfect travel experience for guests.

一、岸上观光部门的职责
The Responsibilities of the Shore Excursion Department

岸上观光部人员需要为宾客设计停靠港的岸上观光游览行程。他们要与当地旅行社、中间商联系,确定游览行程中的交通、观光、购物、用餐、住宿及导游等相关事宜。同时,向宾客介绍并推荐岸上观光行程安排,接受宾客的岸上观光预订。在组织宾客下船参观游览方面,岸上观光部一般与邮轮前台毗邻,配备岸上观光专员,专门为宾客提供咨询解答和预订服务。该部门的人员配置包括岸上观光经理、岸上观光副经理、岸上观光预订专员、导游、私人行程专家、潜水教练等。图5-1为地中海邮轮公司岸上观光宣传页。

The shore excursion team is responsible for designing shore excursion itineraries for guests at the docked ports. They liaise with local travel agencies and intermediaries to arrange aspects such as transportation, sightseeing, shopping, dining, accommodation, and tour guides for the excursions. Simultaneously, they introduce and recommend shore excursion itineraries to guests and accept shore excursion bookings. When it comes to organizing guests to disembark and participate in the excursions, the shore excursion department is typically located adjacent to the cruise reception desk. It is staffed with shore excursion specialists who are dedicated to providing consultation, answers, and booking services to guests. The personnel within this department include shore excursion managers, assistant shore excursion managers, shore excursion booking specialists, tour guides, private itinerary experts, diving instructors, and others. Figure 5-1 shows the shore excursion promotional page of mediterranean cruise line.

图 5-1 地中海邮轮公司岸上观光宣传页

Figure 5-1 Shore Excursion Promotional Page of Mediterranean Cruise Line

二、具体岸上观光部门职责如下
The Specific Responsibilities of the Shore Excursion Department Are as Follows

1.挑选并设计停靠港的岸上观光行程(Selecting and Designing Shore Excursion Itineraries for the Docked Ports)

这一工作需要在邮轮启航前完成。综合考量邮轮在停靠港的停留时间以及成本因素,筛选出停靠港最具代表性的景点、地标建筑、博物馆或热门购物场所,精心设计多条不同的游览线路,以供宾客选择。

This task needs to be completed before the cruise sets sail. By comprehensively considering the duration of the cruise stay at the docked ports and cost factors, screen out the most representative attractions, landmark buildings, museums or popular shopping venues at the docked ports, and meticulously design multiple different tour itineraries for guests to choose from.

2.与陆上旅行社或中间商合作(Collaborating with Land-based Travel Agencies or Intermediaries)

挑选停靠港当地的旅行社或中间商,与其建立合作关系。由当地合作方负责安排导游、交通工具、餐饮住宿等相关事宜。

Select and establish cooperative relationships with local travel agencies or intermediaries at the ports of call, and let the local partners be responsible for arranging tour guides, transportation means, catering, accommodation and other related matters.

3.负责岸上观光的销售（Being Responsible for the Sales of Shore Excursions）

在登船说明会上，由岸上观光专员负责详细介绍不同的游览行程，为宾客提供专业建议，协助宾客选择合适的游览行程。

During the boarding briefing, the shore excursion specialist is responsible for introducing different tour itineraries in detail, providing professional advice to guests, and assisting guests in selecting appropriate tour itineraries.

4.接受宾客岸上观光咨询（Receiving Inquiries from Guests About Shore Excursions）

在宾客登船时，提前准备好岸上观光宣传册。宾客登船后，可前往岸上观光咨询柜台，询问关于陆上行程安排、报价等相关问题。

When guests board the ship, the shore excursion brochures should be prepared in advance. After boarding, guests can go to the shore excursion information counter to inquire about land tour arrangements, quotations and other related issues.

5.接受岸上观光预订（Accepting Bookings for Shore Excursions）

宾客既可以在预订邮轮航线时直接选择岸上观光行程，也可以在登船后，前往岸上观光咨询柜台现场预订停靠港的岸上游览行程。

Guests can either directly choose shore excursion itineraries when booking their cruise tickets or go to the shore excursion information counter on-site after boarding the ship to book shore excursions for the docked ports.

6.打印岸上观光游览票（Print Shore Excursion Tickets）

宾客完成预订后，打印出所有宾客所预订的岸上观光游览票。票据上需清晰印有宾客选择的行程、价格、集合时间和地点、乘坐的交通工具等详细信息。

After guests complete their bookings, print out the shore excursion tickets for all the guests who have made reservations. The tickets should clearly indicate detailed information such as the itinerary selected by the guests, the price, the gathering time and place, the mode of transportation, etc.

7.与相关部门联系通知参加岸上观光的人数（Contacting Relevant Departments to Notify Them of the Number of Participants for Shore Excursions）

与旅行社、中间商等相关部门沟通，及时告知对方参与岸上观光游览项目的人数，以便其合理安排导游、大巴、住宿和餐饮等工作。同时，还要将下船参与岸上观光的人数通知给主厨、餐厅经理、廊桥及酒店经理，方便主厨和餐厅经理确定船上饮食的供应量，以及廊桥和酒店经理根据下船人数确定开放廊桥的数量。

Communicate with relevant departments such as travel agencies and intermediaries, and promptly inform them of the number of people participating in the shore excursion tours, so that they can reasonably arrange tour guides, coaches, accommodation and catering, etc. At the same time, also notify the chef, the restaurant manager, the gangway staff and the hotel manager of the number of people disembarking for shore excursions, so as to help the chef and the restaurant manager determine the quantity of food and beverages on board, and enable the gangway staff and the hotel manager to determine the number of gangways to be opened according to the number of people disembarking.

8.为宾客做好后勤工作（Provide Logistical Support for Guests）

负责协调宾客与旅行社之间的关系，组织宾客按顺序上下船，妥善处理宾客的投诉等问题。

Be responsible for coordinating the relationship between guests and travel agencies, organizing guests to board and disembark in an orderly manner, and properly handling guests' complaints and other issues.

9.为宾客定制个性化岸上观光线路（Customizing Personalized Shore Excursion Itineraries for Guests）

大多数邮轮为宾客提供个性化岸上观光线路。作为个性化旅行的先行者，银海邮轮在提供个性化线路方面表现尤为出色，其陆上观光线路设计专家会依据宾客的喜好量身定制个性化线路。图5-2为岸上观光线路介绍。

Most cruise ships offer personalized shore excursion itineraries for guests. As a pioneer in personalized travel, Silversea Cruises performs particularly well in providing customized itineraries. The land tour itinerary designers will tailor personalized itineraries according to the preferences of guests. Figure 5-2 shows the introduction to shore excursion itineraries.

图 5-2　岸上观光线路介绍

Figure 5-2　Introduction to Shore Excursion Itineraries

实训任务考核指南
Training Task Assessment Guide

实训任务 Training Task	分值(分) Score (Points)	实际得分 Actual Score
仪容仪表、礼貌礼节 Grooming, Politeness and Etiquette	10	
操作程序 Operating Procedure	20	
操作动作 Operating Action	20	
操作质量 Operating Quality	40	
操作时间 Operating Time	10	
【合计】 Total	100	

任务2　组织岸上观光行程
Mission 2　Organize Shore Excursion Itineraries

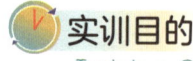

实训目的
Training Objectives

通过教师对岸上观光预定步骤、岸上观光组织过程程序及操作要求的讲解，以及学生开展的岸上观光组织训练，让学生了解并掌握为宾客提供岸上观光服务的步骤和流程，从而达到熟知操作程序与操作规范的训练要求。

Through the teacher's explanation of the reservation procedures, the organizational process, and the operational requirements for shore excursions, and the students' training in organizing shore excursions, the students will understand and master the steps and processes of providing shore-excursion services to guests, thus enabling them to meet the training requirements of being familiar with the operational procedures and norms.

实训方法
Training Method

首先,教师进行示范讲解,随后学生开展动手操作训练。在学生操作训练期间,教师全程指导,学生通过反复强化练习,以实现熟练掌握该项操作技能的目标。

Firstly, the teacher gives a demonstration and explanation, and then the students carry out hands-on practice. During the operation training, the teacher gives guidance, and the students carry out repeated intensive training to achieve the goal of mastering the operation skills.

实训准备
Training Preparation

白板、白板笔、分组讨论任务单、实训手册等。

Whiteboard, whiteboard markers, group discussion task sheets, practical training manuals, etc.

实训内容及操作标准
Training Content and Operating Standards

作为一名合格的邮轮前厅服务员,需具备扎实的前厅服务理论知识。邮轮公司积极鼓励宾客预订由邮轮提供的岸上观光服务,宾客既可以在邮轮航行期间直接预订,也能够在出发前提前预订。通过实训,旨在让学生掌握岸上观光的预订渠道与步骤,熟悉岸上观光的组织流程。

As a qualified cruise ship front desk attendant, he or she must possess solid theoretical knowledge of front desk services. Cruise companies encourage guests to book the shore excursions offered by the cruise ship, which can be done directly on board or in advance before departure. Through practical training, students will master the channels for and steps of booking shore excursions and become familiar with the organization process of shore excursions.

一、岸上观光行程的组织
Organization of Shore Excursion Itineraries

岸上观光行程的组织极大地考验着工作人员的服务水平。工作人员需要与邮轮登船部、餐饮部、港口海关、岸上旅行社等多方面进行协调沟通,以确保宾客岸上观光行程顺利开展。图5-3为岸上观光咨询台。

The organization of shore excursion itineraries greatly tests the staff's service level. Staff members need to coordinate and communicate with various departments such as the boarding department, dining department, port customs, and shore travel agencies to ensure the smooth progress of guests' shore excursions. Figure 5-3 shows the shore excursion information desk.

图 5-3 岸上观光咨询台

Figure 5-3　Shore Excursion Information Desk

1.集合领取交通票（Gather to Collect Transportation Tickets）

岸上观光一般在早餐后集合出发，集合地点通常选定在邮轮的大剧院。不同路线的观光团队会分别张贴不同颜色的标记，具体集合时间和地点需参照当天的安排。

Shore excursions usually depart after breakfast, with the gathering place typically set in the cruise ship's theater. Different tour groups for different itineraries will be labeled with different colors. The specific gathering time and location should refer to the schedule of the day.

出游时，豪华大巴是主要的交通工具，因此宾客需要领取乘车票，乘车票上标有所搭乘车辆的具体信息。在无法停靠大型邮轮的浅水港口，宾客需搭乘接驳船，所以此时需要领取接驳船票。

Luxury buses are the primary mode of transportation for shore excursions, so guests need to collect their bus tickets, which contain specific information about the bus they will be boarding. In shallow water ports where large cruise ships cannot dock, guests need to take a shuttle boat, so they need to collect their shuttle boat tickets.

2.组织宾客入境过关（Organize Guests' Immigration and Customs Clearance）

工作人员要依据各停靠港的入境要求，指导宾客填写入境卡，随后宾客出示护照和签证办理入境手续即可。国内宾客赴日韩邮轮旅游时，上岸流程相对简便，只需在护照复印件上粘贴上岸许可证，返回船上时将其交回。

Staff should guide guests to complete the entry card according to the entry requirements of each port of call, and then guests present their passports and visas for immigration clearance. For domestic guests taking a cruise to Japan or R.O. Korea, the shore-landing process is relatively simple. They only need to attach a departure permit to a copy of their passport, and return the permit when boarding the ship again.

3.引导并组织宾客登车（Guide and Organize Guests to Board the Vehicle）

宾客下船后，会有工作人员引导并组织他们前往停车场登车。

After disembarking from the ship, guests will be guided and organized by staff to board the vehicles at the parking lot.

4. 游览完毕及时返回船上(Return to the Ship Promptly after the Tour)

工作人员需提前告知宾客返程时间,并在游览接近尾声时做好提醒工作,保证宾客能及时返回船上,避免耽误邮轮行程。

Staff need to inform guests of the return time in advance and remind them when the tour is nearly over to ensure that guests can return to the ship in time and avoid delaying the cruise itinerary.

5. 岸上观光行程的评价(Evaluation of Shore Excursion Itineraries)

邮轮行程结束的前一天晚上,客舱服务员会在每间客舱发放一份旅游满意度调查表,宾客需对邮轮本身、邮轮服务、邮轮设施及岸上观光的满意度进行打分。岸上观光工作人员可通过该表格了解宾客对岸上观光行程的满意程度。

On the evening before the end of the cruise, the cabin attendant will distribute a guest satisfaction survey form in each cabin. The guests need to rate their satisfaction with the cruise itself, cruise services, cruise facilities, and shore excursions. The shore excursion staff can use this form to understand the guests' satisfaction with the shore excursion itineraries.

实训任务考核指南
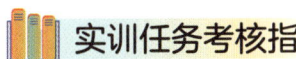
Training Task Assessment Guide

实训任务 Training Task	分值(分) Score(Points)	实际得分 Actual Score
仪容仪表、礼貌礼节 Grooming, Politeness and Etiquette	10	
操作程序 Operating Procedure	20	
操作动作 Operating Action	20	
操作质量 Operating Quality	40	
操作时间 Operating Time	10	
【合计】 Total	100	

项目 2　岸上观光服务常见问题处理
Project 2　Handling Common Issues in Shore Excursion Services

任务 1　常见案例分享
Mission 1　Common Case Sharing

实训目的
Training Objectives

通过教师对岸上观光服务中突发事件,诸如岸上观光行程变更或取消等常见问题处理操作要求的讲解,以及学生围绕岸上观光特殊事件展开的训练,让学生理解并掌握特殊事件的处理方法与步骤流程,进而达到熟知操作程序与操作规范的训练要求。

Through the teacher's explanation of emergency situations in shore excursion services, such as the handling and operational requirements for common issues like changes or cancellations to shore excursion itineraries, as well as through students' training on handling special shore excursion-related events, students will comprehend and master the methods and steps for dealing with these special events. Such training and learning will enable them to meet the training requirements of being familiar with the operational procedures and regulations.

实训方法
Training Method

首先,教师开展示范讲解。随后,学生着手进行动手操作训练。在学生操作训练期间,教师全程予以指导,学生通过反复开展强化训练,以达成熟练掌握该项操作技能的目标。

Firstly, the teacher gives a demonstration and provides an explanation, and then the students carry out hands-on practice. During the students operation training, the teacher gives guidance, and the students conduct repeated intensive training to achieve the goal of mastering the operation skills.

实训准备
Training Preparation

白板、白板笔、分组讨论任务单、实训手册等。

Whiteboard, whiteboard markers, group discussion task sheets, practical training manuals, etc.

实训内容及操作标准
Training Content and Operating Standards

作为一名合格的邮轮前厅服务员,需具备扎实的前厅服务理论知识。当邮轮公司因不可抗力等因素变更或取消行程时,服务员需要及时向宾客做出解释,并采取相应措施。通过实训,旨在让学生掌握岸上观光组织过程中突发事件的处理方法与步骤,使其能够应对岸上观光服务中的常见问题。

As a qualified cruise ship front desk attendant, he or she must possess solid theoretical knowledge of front desk services. When cruise companies change or cancel itineraries due to force majeure and other factors, the front desk attendant must promptly explain the situation to guests and take corresponding measures. Through practical training, students will master the methods and steps for handling emergencies in shore excursion organization and be able to deal with common issues encountered in shore excursion services.

一、常见案例分享

Common Case Studies Sharing

1. 岸上观光活动计划变更的处理(Handling Changes in Shore Excursion Activity Plans)

夏秋两季,太平洋航线常遭遇台风,加勒比海航线则常受飓风侵袭。遇此情形,出于安全考量,小型邮轮可能会延迟启航,甚至取消航行或变更目的地;而大型邮轮,若台风强度未达极端,航次通常会继续,只是可能会调整停靠港口,或者改变到港顺序。

During the summer and autumn seasons, typhoons frequently hit the Pacific cruise routes, and hurricanes often affect the Caribbean cruise routes. In such cases, for safety reasons, smaller cruise ships may delay their departure, cancel the voyage, or change their destination. However, for larger cruise ships, if the storm is not particularly severe, the cruise will continue, but there may be changes to the ports or the order of port visits.

若在出行前遭遇台风,邮轮公司会提前通知包船方或切舱方,并提供一套或两套解决方案,由旅行社或宾客进行选择并予以确认。

If a typhoon is encountered before departure, the cruise company will notify the charterer or the cabin allocator in advance and provide one or two sets of solutions for the travel agency or guests to choose and confirm.

倘若在行程当中遇到台风,邮轮公司将在船上做出妥善安排。邮轮观光服务部会依据实际状况以及船方提供的信息,及时向宾客通报情况、安抚宾客情绪,同时配合航行部门顺利完成航行任务。

If a typhoon is encountered during the trip, the cruise company will make arrangements on board. The cruise tour service department will promptly notify the guests of the situation and reassure them based on the actual situation and information from the ship, and cooperate with the navigation department to complete the navigation tasks smoothly.

2.误船(Missing the Ship)

当宾客因迷路、走错码头、未能把控好岸上观光时间、记错上船时间等原因误船时,岸上旅游服务商需及时通知船方。邮轮观光服务部若接到误船宾客的求助电话,或者在登记返回邮轮的宾客信息、核对人数过程中发现有宾客误船,应立即向船长和航行部门报告。随后,可根据实际情况采取相应措施,如推迟起航时间;若无法推迟起航,则安排宾客搭乘其他航班,或安排宾客在下一个港口登船,而由此产生的费用需由宾客自行承担。

When guests miss the ship due to getting lost, going to the wrong pier, failing to manage the shore excursion time properly, or remembering the wrong boarding time, the shore tour service provider should promptly notify the ship. If the Cruise Ship Tour Service Department receives a call for help from a guest who has missed the ship, or learns that a guest has missed the ship during the registration and counting of guests returning to the ship, it should promptly report to the captain and the navigation department. The ship may, depending on the situation, either delay its departure; if not possible, arrange for the guest to take another flight or board the ship at the next port. The costs incurred shall be borne by the guest.

3.岸上观光时间缩短的处理(Handling Shortened Shore Excursion Time)

当邮轮晚点抵达码头,而离港时间保持不变时,岸上观光时间将相应缩短。针对这种情况,邮轮观光服务部和团体领队应采取以下应变措施:

When the cruise ship arrives at the pier late while the departure time remains unchanged, the shore excursion time will be correspondingly shortened. In this case, the Cruise Ship Tour Service Department and the group leader should take the following contingency measures:

①与船方充分商讨应急预案,确保双方达成一致。

Fully discuss and reach an agreement on an emergency response plan with the ship's management.

②及时向宾客坦诚说明面临的困难,并致以诚挚歉意。

Promptly explain the situation to the guests and sincerely apologize.

③分别请领队针对每位宾客做好沟通安抚工作。

Request the group leader to individually communicate with and comfort and reassure each guest.

④争分夺秒,确保宾客能够游览计划内的景点。

Seize every minute to ensure that guests can visit the planned attractions.

⑤倘若确实存在困难,应制订应变计划,着重突出本地最具代表性的游览景点。

If it is indeed the case that there are difficulties, develop an alternative plan that highlights the most representative local attractions.

⑥与船方沟通,探讨是否可给予宾客一定补偿,例如发放一些小礼品。

Communicate with the ship's management to see whether any compensation (such as distributing small gifts) can be provided.

4.宾客遗失船卡的处理(Handling Lost Ship Cards for Guests)

邮轮会为每一位登船宾客制作并发放一张船卡。船卡上涵盖宾客姓名、房号、用餐餐厅名称、用餐时间、桌号以及乘船日期等信息。它兼具宾客登船识别证、签账卡以及船舱钥匙的功能。在宾客每次登船以及于船上进行消费时,邮轮工作人员都会要求其出示该船卡。因此,宾客务必将船卡随身携带并妥善保管。宾客上船后,护照会统一交由船方保管,上岸观光或参加其他活动后返回登船时,出示船卡即可。倘若宾客在岸上发现船卡遗失,观光导游及陪同人员首先应让失主冷静回忆,详细了解船卡遗失的具体情形,寻找线索并协助其寻找;若确定船卡已丢失,应立即向船上的观光服务部或宾客服务中心报告,以便船方尽快重新补制船卡。

The cruise ship issues a ship card to every boarding guest, which contains information such as the guest's name, room number, dining restaurant name, meal time, table number, and sailing date. The ship card serves as the guest's boarding identification, charge card, and cabin key. Whenever guests board the ship or make purchases on board, cruise staff will require them to present this ship card. Guests need to properly carry and keep the ship card with them at all times. After guests board the ship, their passports are handed over to the ship's management for safekeeping. When returning to the ship after shore excursions or other activities, guests only need to present their ship cards. If a guest discovers that he or she has lost his or her ship card while ashore, the tour guide and accompanying personnel should first ask the owner to calmly recall the situation and provide detailed information about the loss, locate any clues, and assist in the search. If the ship card is indeed lost, it should be immediately reported to the ship's shore excursion service department or guest service center, so that the ship's management can promptly issue a replacement ship card.

5.宾客在岸上突发意外事故的处理(Handling Unexpected Accidents on Shore for Guests)

若宾客在岸上遭遇重大意外或突发严重病情,岸上旅游服务商有责任联系当地医院,并即刻将宾客送往医院进行抢救,同时及时向船方通报患者的情况。若宾客病情较轻,则可返回船上后再就医。国际邮轮通常配备专门的医务室,医务室中有若干名全科医生和护士,医生会及时对病人进行诊断与处理。倘若宾客购买了个人旅游意外险,应及时联系保险公司,说明保险相关事宜,以便事后回国进行理赔。

If a guest suffers a major accident or severe illness on shore, the shore tour service provider is responsible for contacting the local hospital, promptly transport the patient for medical treatment, and informing the ship's management of the patient's condition. If the illness is not severe, the patient can seek medical attention on board after returning to the ship. International cruise ships are equipped with dedicated medical rooms staffed with several general practitioners and nurses, who will promptly diagnose and treat the patient. If the guest has purchased personal travel accident insurance, he or she should contact the insurance company promptly to explain the insurance details to facilitate the claims process upon returning to their home country.

6.宾客脱逃事件的处理(Handling Incidents of Guest Escape)

在码头集合阶段,邮轮观光服务部工作人员、团体领队以及岸上旅游服务商,都应仔细留意宾客状况。一旦察觉异常,可请边检人员协助询问。若经边检发现问题,边防部门会及时通知船方或当地移民局,此时严禁让相关宾客下船。倘若在旅游行程中出现有人脱逃的情况,团体领队和当地导游务必立即通知船方和旅行社,并及时拟定解决方案予以应对。

During the assembly at the pier, Cruise Ship Tour Service Department staff, group leaders, and shore tour service providers should carefully observe the guests. If any abnormal situations arise, they should request the assistance of border inspection personnel for inquiries. If any issues are discovered by border inspection, the border defense department will notify the ship's management or the local immigration office, and the relevant guests will not be allowed to disembark. If someone escapes during the tour, the group leader and local tour guide should promptly notify the ship's management and the travel agency to formulate timely solutions to deal with the situation.

实训任务考核指南
Training Task Assessment Guide

实训任务 Training Task	分值(分) Score (Points)	实际得分 Actual Score
仪容仪表、礼貌礼节 Grooming, Politeness and Etiquette	10	
操作程序 Operating Procedure	20	
操作动作 Operating Action	20	
操作质量 Operating Quality	40	
操作时间 Operating Time	10	
【合计】 Total	100	

模块 6

未来航程服务

Module 6

Future Cruise Service

项目 1　未来航程线路
Project 1　Future Cruise Itinerary

任务 1　未来航程线路设计
Mission 1　Future Cruise Itinerary Design

实训目的　Training Objectives

通过教师对未来航程线路进行示例讲解,以及学生开展未来航程线路设计训练,让学生理解并掌握未来航程线路设计的要点,从而达到熟知设计要点与设计规范的训练要求。

Through the teacher's explanation of examples of future cruise itineraries and students' participation in the design training of future cruise itineraries, students can understand and master the key points of future cruise itinerary design, and meet the training requirements of being familiar with design points and design specifications.

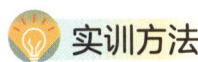
实训方法　Training Method

1.教师示范讲解成熟的航程线路以及航程线路设计要点。

The teacher demonstrates and explains the mature itinerary and the key points of the itinerary design.

2.将学生按 6 人一组进行分组,每组选任一名小组长。小组长前往教师处抽选航区

（预先准备好日韩航区、东南亚航区、北欧航区、澳新航区等七大世界邮轮航线航区）。各小组依据抽选结果，选择一艘该航区最具代表性的邮轮。

Students are grouped into teams of six, and each team selects a leader. The group leader goes to the teacher to draw lots for the cruise region. There are a total of seven world-class cruise regions prepared in advance, such as the Japan-Korea cruise region, Southeast Asia cruise region, Nordic cruise region, and Australia-New Zealand cruise region. Each group selects the most representative cruise ship in the chosen region based on the lottery result.

3.各小组深入研究选定邮轮的航线，按照本小组想要展示的主题，进行契合中国宾客需求的航程线路设计。设计需充分展现航线的主题、亮点、卖点、客源分析、目标客源定位、价格定位等内容，并以PPT形式呈现。完成设计后，各小组进行展示，通过师生、生生之间的研讨与评价，使学生达成熟练掌握该项技能的目标。

Each group carefully studies the route of the selected cruise ship and designs an itinerary suitable for Chinese guests according to the theme their group wants to show. It is required to fully present the theme, highlights, selling points, passenger source analysis, target passenger source positioning, price positioning and other aspects, and present it in the form of a PPT. After completion, each group gives a presentation. Through discussions and evaluations among teachers and students, students can master this skill proficiently.

4.在学生进行航程线路设计过程中，教师予以指导，学生反复对设计进行修改与完善。

During the students' cruise itinerary design process, the teacher offers guidance, and the students repeatedly modify and perfect their designs.

实训准备
Training Preparation

信息：邮轮管理信息系统、电脑、成熟航程线路海报及宣传册等。

Information: Cruise Management Information System, computers, posters and brochures of mature cruise itineraries, etc.

实训内容及操作标准
Training Content and Operating Standards

作为一名合格的邮轮未来航程规划部工作人员，应当熟练掌握未来航程线路的设计要点，并能够独立完成简单的未来航程线路设计。具体操作流程如下：

As a qualified staff member of the cruise ship future itinerary planning department, one should master the key points of future cruise itinerary design proficiently and be capable of independently completing simple future cruise itinerary designs. The specific operation procedures are as follows:

未来航程线路设计程序
Future Cruise Itinerary Design Program

1. 邮轮原有航程线路研讨（Discussion on the Original Itinerary of the Cruise Ship）

依据邮轮原有的航程线路，深入研究邮轮停靠母港的旅游资源环境、地缘空间位置等实际状况，将这些研究成果作为新航线邮轮停靠母港选择的重要依据。

Based on the original itinerary of the cruise ship, conduct an in-depth study of the tourism resource environment, geospatial location and other actual conditions of the cruise ship's home port. The research results will be used as an important basis for choosing the home port of the new cruise itinerary.

2. 市场需求和消费者心理研究（Research on Market Demand and Consumer Psychology）

着重分析目标宾客群体的旅游欲望、风俗习惯、地缘政治因素、历史文化背景以及消费能力等相关内容，以此作为航线设计的重要参考依据。

Focus on analyzing the tourism desires, customs, geopolitical factors, historical and cultural backgrounds, and consumption capabilities of the target customer groups, using these as important references for route design.

3. 未来航程线路主题确定（The Theme of the Future Cruise Itinerary is Determined）

基于邮轮自身原有的航程线路、目标宾客群体的需求与欲望，以及邮轮母港周边的旅游资源环境、地缘空间位置等现实条件，获取邮轮航线设计的思路灵感，进而最终确定未来航程线路的主题。

Based on the original cruise itinerary of the cruise ship itself, the needs and desires of the target customer group, as well as the tourism resource environment and geospatial location around the cruise home port and other actual conditions, obtain inspiration for the design of the cruise route, and ultimately determine the theme of the future cruise itinerary.

4. 未来航程线路设计初探（Preliminary Exploration of Future Itinerary Design）

根据未来航程线路的主题、对原有航程线路的研讨结果以及对目标宾客群体特点的分析，进行邮轮停靠母港的筛选，并初步规划出航程线路。

Based on the theme of the future cruise itinerary, the research results of the original cruise itinerary, and the analysis of the characteristics of the target customer group, select the cruise ship's home port and preliminarily plan the cruise itinerary.

5. 停靠母港旅游产品确定（Determination of Tourism Products at the Home Port）

结合目标宾客群体分析结果、邮轮母港的旅游资源情况以及地缘空间位置等实际状况，依据目的地的文化和地理环境，对岸上旅游资源进行整合，设计出适合的岸上观光产品。

Combining the analysis results of the target customer group, the tourism resources of the cruise home port, and the geospatial location and other actual conditions, integrate the on-shore tourism resources according to the cultural and geographical environment of the destination, and design suitable on-shore sightseeing products.

6.合理的线路行程规划制定(Reasonable Itinerary Planning)

基于未来航程线路设计的初步成果以及邮轮母港岸上观光线路设计方案,进行每日行程的规划安排。

Based on the preliminary results of the future cruise itinerary design and the design of the on-shore sightseeing routes at the cruise home port, plan the daily itinerary.

7.未来航程线路定价(Future Cruise Itinerary Pricing)

参考原有航程线路的价格以及目标宾客群体的消费水平,对新航程线路进行成本核算,从而确定新线路的最终定价。尤其要对销售量、成本和利润的预估进行复审,以确定这些指标是否能够满足邮轮公司的效益目标。

Refer to the prices of the original cruise itinerary and the consumption levels of the target customer group to calculate the costs of the new cruise itinerary, thereby determining the final price of the new route. In particular, review the forecasts of sales volume, costs, and profits to determine whether these indicators can meet the benefit goals of the cruise company.

未来航程线路设计图解
Step Diagram of Future Cruise Itinerary Design

1.航线研讨
Itinerary Discussion

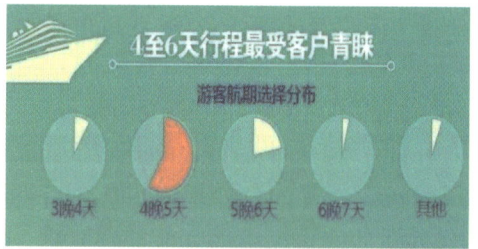

2.目标群体分析
Target Group Analysis

3.主题确定
Theme Determined

4.航线初探
Preliminary Exploration of the Itinerary

模块6 未来航程服务
Module 6 Future Cruise Service

5. 岸上观光
Shore Sightseeing

6. 行程规划
Itinerary Planning

7. 航线定价
Itinerary Pricing

实训任务考核指南
Training Task Assessment Guide

实训任务 Training Task	分值（分） Score（Points）	实际得分 Actual Score
仪容仪表、礼貌礼节 Grooming, Politeness and Etiquette	10	
设计合理性 Design Reasonability	20	
设计可行性 Design Feasibility	20	
设计特色 Design Features	40	
成本核算 Cost Accounting	10	
【合计】 Total	100	

项目 2 未来航程销售
Project 2 Future Cruise Sales

任务 1 未来航程推介
Mission 1 Future Cruise Promotion

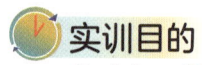
实训目的
Training Objectives

教师对未来航程销售程序和技巧进行讲解,并安排学生开展对未来航程的推介训练,让学生了解和掌握未来航程销售的要点,以达到熟知销售程序与技巧的训练要求。

Through the teacher's explanation of the sales procedures and techniques for future cruises and the students' promotional training on future cruises, the students can understand and master the key points of future cruise sales, thus meeting the training requirements of being familiar with the sales procedures and techniques.

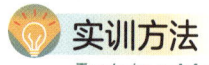
实训方法
Training Method

1.教师示范讲解未来航程的销售程序与技巧。
The teacher demonstrates and explains the sales procedures and skills of future cruises.

2.学生依据此前的分组,在课下围绕先前设计的未来航程线路,制作宣传海报与宣传视频。在课上进行未来航程推介时,需以 PPT、宣传海报以及宣传视频相结合的形式呈现,要求全面展示航线的主题、亮点、卖点、客源分析、目标客源定位、价格定位等内容。小组展示完毕后,展开师生、生生之间的研讨评价,以此达到熟练掌握该项技能的目的。

According to the previous grouping, students will create publicity posters and promotional videos for the previously designed future cruise routes after class. During the in-class promotion of future cruises, it should be presented in the form of a combination of PPT, publicity posters and promotional videos. It is required to comprehensively display the theme, highlights, selling points of the routes, passenger source analysis, target passenger source positioning, price positioning and other contents. After the group presentations, discussions and evaluations among teachers and students, as well as among students themselves, are carried out to achieve the goal of mastering this skill proficiently.

3.此次推介面向全班同学,每个小组均有5分钟时间,向作为意向宾客的其他同学进行一对一推介。推介结束后进行投票,每名同学仅有一次投票权,需投给自己中意的航程。每组最终得票数按比例折算为实训分,得票最多的小组获10分,第二名获9分,以此类推。

This promotion is targeted at the whole class. Each group has five minutes to conduct a one-on-one promotion to other classmates who act as potential customers. After the promotion, a vote will be held. Each student has only one vote and needs to vote for their favorite cruise. The final number of votes for each group is converted into practical training scores proportionally. The group with the most votes gets 10 points, the second-placed group gets 9 points, and so on.

实训准备
Training Preparation

信息:电脑、宣传海报、PPT、宣传视频、未来航程预订表等。

Information: computers, promotional posters, PPT, promotional videos, future cruise reservation forms, etc.

实训内容及操作标准
Training Content and Operating Standards

作为一名合格的邮轮未来航程部服务员,应熟练掌握未来航程的销售程序与技巧,能够熟练地开展未来航程推介工作。其具体内容如下:

As a qualified attendant in the Future Cruise Department of a cruise ship, one should be proficient in the sales procedures and skills of future cruises and be able to conduct future cruise promotion work proficiently. The specific contents are as follows:

一、未来航程销售程序和技巧
Future Cruise Sales Procedures and Skills

1. 明确未来航程销售的内容（Clarify the Content of Future Cruise Sales）

未来航程销售的内容包括邮轮的设施设备、邮轮的服务、邮轮的航线、邮轮的氛围、邮轮的形象等。

The content of future cruise sales includes the facilities and equipment of the cruise ship, the services on the cruise ship, the cruise itineraries, the atmosphere on the cruise ship, the image of the cruise ship, etc.

2. 做好未来航程销售的准备（Prepare for Future Cruise Sales）

（1）掌握邮轮航线和客舱的基本情况。

Master the basic information about cruise itineraries and cabins.

（2）熟悉竞争对手的产品状况

Be familiar with the product status of competitors

了解竞争对手产品的基础上帮助宾客做有效的比较，凸显自身产品的特色和亮点、性价比、服务等。

On the basis of understanding competitors' products, help guests make effective comparisons and highlight the features and highlights, cost-effectiveness, services, etc.

（3）了解不同宾客的心理需求

Understand the psychological needs of different guests

重点了解目标宾客群体的旅游欲望、风俗人情、国缘政治、历史文化、消费能力等相关内容，在此基础上引导宾客消费。

Focus on understanding the travel desires, customs, geopolitical situations, historical cultures, consumption capabilities and other relevant aspects of the target customer group, and guide guests to consume based on this.

（4）表现出良好的职业素质

Demonstrate good professional qualities

销售人员在销售之前要确保有足够的知识储量，信息包括邮轮公司、品牌、船只、航线、停靠港目的地等，在销售过程中要准确地表达航程的相关内容，并与宾客保持良好的沟通。

Sales staff should ensure sufficient knowledge reserves before selling, including information about cruise companies, brands, ships, itineraries, port-of-call destinations, etc. During the sales process, they should accurately convey the relevant details of the cruise and maintain good communication with guests.

3.遵循未来航程销售的流程(Follow the Process of Future Cruise Sales)

(1)提供各种航线宣传资料。
Provide various publicity materials for cruise itineraries.
(2)介绍航线和客舱。
Introduce cruise itineraries and cabins.
(3)提供专业的未来航程和停靠港目的地的旅游建议。
Provide professional travel advice for future cruises and port-of-call destinations.
(4)提供未来航程咨询服务,解答宾客有关未来航程的相关问题。
Provide future cruise consultation services and answer guests' questions related to future cruises.
(5)根据宾客需要制订未来航程旅行计划。
Develop future cruise travel plans according to guests' needs.
(6)说明优惠,促成预订。
Explain preferential offers and facilitate reservations.
(7)熟知未来航程预订计划以帮助宾客填写未来航程预订表并接受预订。
Be familiar with the future cruise reservation plan to assist guests in filling out the future cruise reservation form and accept reservations.

实训任务考核指南

Training Task Assessment Guide

实训任务 Training Task	分值(分) Score (Points)	实际得分 Actual Score
仪容仪表、礼貌礼节 Grooming, Politeness and Etiquette	10	
未来航程销售准备 Prepare for Future Cruise Sales	20	
未来航程销售技巧 Skill for Future Cruise Sales	20	
未来航程销售程序 Procedure for Future Cruise Sales	40	
未来航程销售成交量排名 Turnover Ranking for Future Cruise Sales	10	
【合计】 Total	100	

任务 2 未来航程舱房推介
Mission 2
Future Cruise Cabin Promotion

实训目的 Training Objectives

通过教师对未来航程舱房销售程序和技巧的讲解,并组织学生开展对未来航程舱房的推介训练,让学生了解和掌握未来航程舱房销售的要点,以达到熟知销售程序与技巧的训练要求。

Through the teacher's explanation of the sales procedures and techniques for future cruise cabins and the organization of students to carry out promotional training for future cruise cabins, students can understand and master the key points of future cruise cabin sales, thus meeting the training requirements of being familiar with the sales procedures and skills.

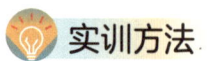
实训方法 Training Method

1.教师示范讲解未来航程舱房的销售程序与技巧。

The teacher demonstrates and explains the sales procedures and skills of future cruise cabins.

2.学生依据之前的分组,在课下围绕先前设计的未来航程线路所选定的邮轮,制作舱房宣传海报及 PPT。在课上进行舱房推介时,需以 PPT 与宣传海报相结合的形式呈现,要求全面展示舱房的亮点、卖点、价格定位、优惠政策等内容。小组展示结束后,开展师生之间以及生生之间的研讨评价,以此达成熟练掌握该项技能的目标。

According to the previous grouping, students will create cabin publicity posters and PPTs for the cruise ships selected in the previously designed future cruise routes after class. When promoting the cabins in class, they should present in the form of a combination of PPTs and publicity posters. It is required to comprehensively display the highlights, selling points, price positioning, preferential policies, etc. of the cabins. After the group presentations, discussions and evaluations among teachers and students, as well as among students themselves, will be carried out to achieve the goal of mastering this skill proficiently.

3.此次推介面向全班同学,每个小组有 10 分钟时间,向作为意向宾客的其他同学进行一对一的报价及推介。推介结束后进行投票，每名同学仅有一次投票权，需投给自己中意的邮轮舱房推介方案。每组最终得票数按比例折算为实训分，得票最多的小组获10分，第二名获9分，以此类推。

This promotion is targeted at the whole class. Each group has ten minutes to conduct a one-on-one quotation and promotion to other classmates who act as potential customers. After the promotion, a vote will be held. Each student has only one vote and needs to vote for their favorite cruise cabin promotion plan. The final number of votes for each group is converted into practical training scores proportionally. The group with the most votes gets 10 points, the second-placed group gets 9 points, and so on.

实训准备
Training Preparation

信息：电脑、宣传海报、PPT等。
Information: computers, promotional posters, PPT, etc.

实训内容及操作标准
Training Content and Operating Standards

作为一名合格的邮轮未来航程部服务员，应当熟练掌握未来航程舱房的销售程序与技巧，能够熟练地开展未来航程舱房销售工作。其具体内容如下：

As a qualified future cruise department staff of a cruise ship, one should be proficient in the sales procedures and skills of future cruise cabins and be proficient in conducting future cruise cabin sales work. The specific contents are as follows:

一、未来航程舱房销售程序和技巧
Future Cruise Cabin Sales Procedures and Techniques

1.做好舱房销售准备（Prepare for Cabin Sales）

（1）掌握邮轮的舱房种类
Master the types of cabins of cruise ships

邮轮的舱房一般分为内舱房、海景房、阳台房和套房。在开展舱房销售前，销售人员应全面掌握每种舱房类型的规格等级、可容纳宾客数量、相应的配套服务设施以及特殊房型，从而为宾客提供充分且多样化的选择。

The cabins on cruise ships are generally classified into inside cabins, ocean-view rooms, balcony rooms, and suites. Before engaging in cabin sales, sales staff should fully understand the specifications and grades of each cabin type, the number of guests it can accommodate, the corresponding supporting service facilities, and special cabin types, so as to provide guests with abundant and diverse choices.

（2）掌握邮轮舱房房态

Master the status of cruise cabins

邮轮舱房的房态通常有可出租房、走客房、已做住客房、未做住客房、维修房、自用房、保留房、双锁房、请勿打扰房和请即打扫房等。在进行舱房销售前，销售人员必须充分熟悉相关房态，防止出现超额订房的情况。

The status of cruise cabins usually includes available for rent rooms, check-out rooms, occupied clean rooms, occupied dirty rooms, out-of-order rooms, staff use rooms, reserved rooms, double-locked rooms, do-not-disturb rooms, and please-clean-immediately rooms, etc. Before cabin sales, sales staff must be fully familiar with the relevant room status to avoid overbooking.

（3）掌握邮轮舱房价格

Master the prices of cruise cabins

由于邮轮舱房各不相同，价格也存在较大差异。在舱房销售前，销售人员应牢记相关价格以及优惠政策等信息，以便在宾客咨询时能快速准确地回应，助力宾客做出选择。

Since cruise cabins vary, there are significant differences in prices. Before selling cabins, sales staff should remember relevant price information and preferential policies, etc., so as to respond quickly and accurately when guests make inquiries and help guests make choices.

2.了解宾客需求(Understand Guest Needs)

员工需要深入了解宾客的需求与期望。比如，宾客是期望体验高档舱房的优质服务，还是更倾向于居住空间更加宽敞的舱房。通过掌握这些信息，便于后续有针对性地为宾客推荐合适的舱房。

Employees need to deeply understand the needs and expectations of customers. For example, whether customers expect to experience the high-quality service of high-end cabins or prefer more spacious cabins. By grasping this information, it is convenient to subsequently recommend suitable cabins to customers in a targeted manner.

3.判断宾客定位(Determine the Guest's Positioning)

销售人员应依据宾客的身份和地位，合理推断其可能选择的客房类型，为精准进行舱房推介提供有力依据。

Sales staff should reasonably infer the possible types of cabins that customers may choose based on their identities and statuses, providing a strong basis for accurate cabin promotion.

4.介绍舱房优点(Introduce the Advantages of the Cabin)

在向宾客介绍舱房时，销售人员要着重强调舱房的独特卖点，如迷人的景观、完备的设施、贴心的配套服务等，以此激发宾客的兴趣。

When introducing cabins to customers, sales staff should emphasize the unique selling points of cabins, such as charming views, complete facilities, attentive supporting services, etc., to stimulate customers' interest.

5. 运用报价技巧，灵活报价（Apply Quotation Skills and Quote Flexibly）

（1）调整舱房报价顺序

Adjust the quotation sequence of cabins

对于身份地位较高或对价格不太在意的宾客，可采用从低到高的报价方式；针对价格敏感型宾客，以及那些存在选择困难的宾客，宜采取交叉排列的报价方式，即先报最低房价，接着报最高房价，最后报中间档次的房价。这种报价方法能给予宾客更多样化的选择机会。

For guests with high status or those who don't care much about prices, the quotation method from low to high can be adopted. For price-sensitive guests and those who have difficulty making choices, the cross-arranged quotation method is advisable, that is, first quote the lowest room rate, then the highest room rate, and finally the middle-level room rate. This quotation method can provide guests with more diverse options.

（2）灵活舱房报价方式

Be flexible in cabin quotation methods

针对不同类型的舱房，应采用不同的报价方式。对于价格较为低廉的低档客舱，可采用冲击式报价，即先直接报出价格，随后介绍客舱情况；对于价格昂贵的高档客舱，适合采用鱼尾式报价，即先详细介绍客舱的优势，之后再给出价格；而对于中档客舱，则可采取三明治式报价，即先进行介绍，接着报价，最后再补充介绍一些客舱亮点。

For different types of cabins, different quotation methods should be used. For low-cost and low-grade cabins, the impact quotation method can be adopted, that is, first quote the price directly and then introduce the cabin. For expensive high-end cabins, the fishtail quotation method is suitable, that is, first introduce the advantages of the cabin in detail and then give the price. For mid-range cabins, the sandwich quotation method can be adopted, that is, first introduce, then quote, and finally introduce some more highlights of the cabin.

6. 实时捕捉宾客反映，达成交易（Capture Guest Feedback in Real Time and Conclude Transactions）

在舱房推介过程中，销售人员要善于实时捕捉宾客的反应，在合适的时机替宾客做出决策，推动交易达成。

During the cabin promotion process, sales staff should be good at capturing guests' reactions in real-time and make decisions for guests at the right time to promote the conclusion of transactions.

实训任务考核指南
Training Task Assessment Guide

实训任务 Training Task	分值(分) Score（Points）	实际得分 Actual Score
仪容仪表、礼貌礼节 Grooming, Politeness and Etiquette	10	
未来航程舱房销售准备 Prepare for Future Cruise Cabin Sales	20	
未来航程舱房销售技巧 Skill for Future Cruise Cabin Sales	20	
未来航程舱房销售程序 Procedure for Future Cruise Cabin Sales	40	
未来航程舱房销售成交量排名 Turnover Ranking for Future Cruise Cabin Sales	10	
【合计】 Total	100	

未来航船预订 项目 3
Future Ship Reservation Project 3

任务 1 未来航程船票预订
Mission 1
Reservations for Future Cruise Tickets

实训目的
Training Objectives

通过教师对未来航程船票预订程序的示范讲解,并组织学生开展未来航程船票的预订训练,让学生了解和掌握未来航程船票预订程序,从而达到熟知操作程序与操作规范的训练要求。

Through the teacher's demonstration and explanation of the reservations for future cruise tickets procedures and the organization of students to carry out future cruise ticket-booking training, students can understand and master the future cruise ticket-booking procedures, thus meeting the training requirements of being familiar with the operating procedures and operating specifications.

实训方法
Training Method

首先,教师进行示范讲解。随后,学生模拟宾客身份,开展不同渠道的未来航程船票预订操作训练。在学生模拟训练期间,教师予以指导,学生通过反复强化训练,以达到熟练掌握该项操作技能的目的。

First, the teacher demonstrates and explains. Subsequently, students simulate the roles of guests and conduct reservation operation training for future cruise tickets through different channels. During the students' simulation training, the teacher offers guidance, and the students carry out repeated intensive training to achieve the goal of proficiently mastering this operational skill.

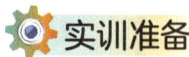

实训准备
Training Preparation

信息：手机、电脑等。

Information: mobile phones, computers, etc.

实训内容及操作标准
Training Content and Operating Standards

作为一名合格的邮轮未来航程部服务员,应当熟练掌握未来航程船票预订程序,能够熟练地开展未来航程船票预订工作。具体程序如下：

As a qualified staff member in the Future Cruise Department of a cruise ship, one should be proficient in the booking procedures for future cruise tickets and be able to skillfully carry out the work of booking future cruise tickets. The specific procedures are as follows:

一、未来航程船票预订的程序
Procedures for Booking Tickets for Future Cruises

1.线下预订流程(Offline Booking Process)

(1)咨询相关公司(旅行社、邮轮公司等)。

Consult relevant companies (such as travel agencies, cruise companies, etc.).

(2)根据自身需求选择邮轮产品。

Select cruise products based on your own requirements.

(3)提交出游人的相关资料。

Submit relevant information of the travelers.

(4)确定船票金额并付款。

Determine the ticket amount and make the payment.

(5)仔细研读订单相关条款并签订合同。

Carefully read the relevant terms of the order and sign the contract.

(6)明确取消条款。

Clarify the cancellation terms.

(7)做好出行攻略。

Prepare a good travel plan.

2.在线预订流程(Online Booking Process)

(1)线上浏览邮轮产品。
Browse cruise products online.
(2)根据自身需求选择邮轮产品。
Select cruise products according to your own needs.
(3)填写出游人的相关信息。
Fill in the relevant information of the travelers.
(4)确认订单并提交。
Confirm the order and submit it.
(5)在线支付订单费用。
Pay the order fees online.
(6)仔细研读订单相关条款并签订在线合同。
Carefully read the relevant terms of the order and sign the online contract.
(7)明确取消条款。
Clarify the cancellation terms.
(8)做好出行攻略。
Prepare a good travel plan.

未来航程船票预订的程序图解(以同程旅游为例)
Step Diagram of the Procedure for Booking Tickets for Future Cruises
(Taking Tongcheng Travel Holdings Limited as an Example)

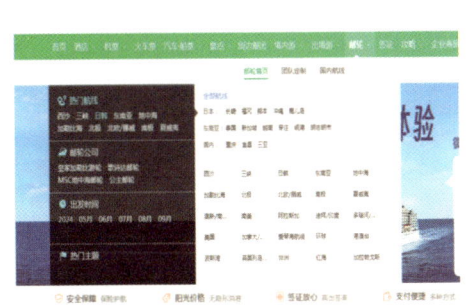

1.选择邮轮航线
Choose a Cruise Itinerary

2.选择邮轮航次
Choose a Cruise Ship

3.确定合适行程与产品
Determine the Appropriate Itinerary and Products

4.查看行程
Check the Itinerary

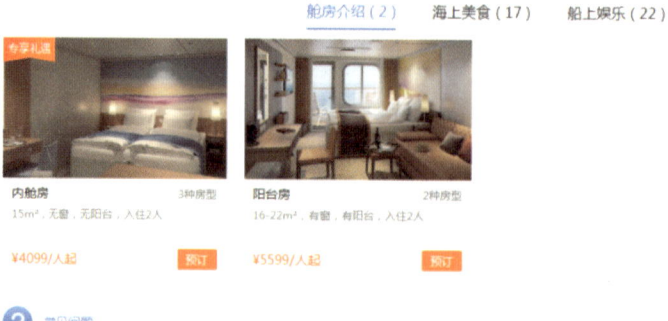

5.选择需要的房型
Choose the Room Type You Need

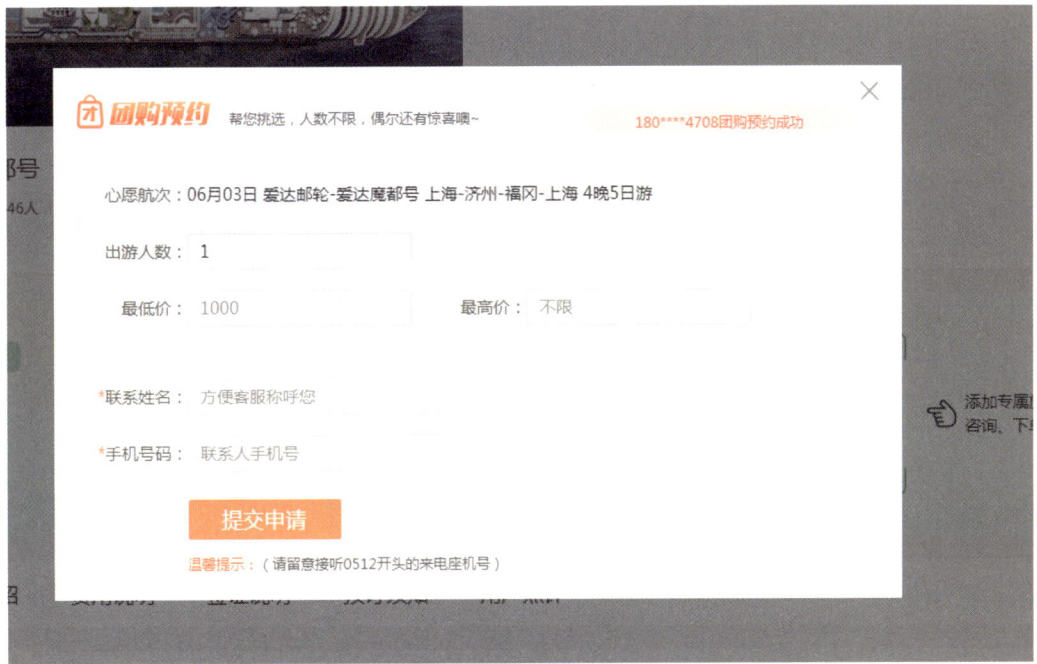

6.填写联系人、出游人信息

Fill in the Contact Person and Traveler Information

支付方式

网上支付： 1、下载同程旅游APP进行预订支付.
2、登陆同程旅游网站进行预订支付.

支持：
微信　　支付宝　　网上银行　　信用卡　　银联

门市支付： 门市刷卡（为了您的支付方便和安全性，请优先选择刷卡支付）、转账支票、现金支付

7.提交订单并在线支付

Submit the Order and Pay Online

签约方式

邮件签约　　　　　　　　　　　　门市签约

我们会将盖章的电子合同发送到您指定的电子邮箱，在收到邮件后请及时　　前往同程设在各城市的门店进行线下签约付款.
阅读合同及相关附件，并回复"已阅，同意签约"完成签约流程.

8.签订合同

Sign the Contract

实训任务考核指南
Training Task Assessment Guide

实训任务 Training Task	分值(分) Score（Points）	实际得分 Actual Score
仪容仪表、礼貌礼节 Grooming, Politeness and Etiquette	10	
操作程序 Operating Procedure	20	
操作动作 Operating Action	20	
操作质量 Operating Quality	40	
操作时间 Operating Time	10	
【合计】 Total	100	

模块 7

邮轮收银服务

Module 7

Cruise Bill Settlement

项目 1 邮轮收银基础
Project 1 Foundation of Cruise Bill Settlement

任务 1 外币真假鉴别
Mission 1 Identification of Foreign Currency Authenticity

实训目的 Training Objectives

本任务聚焦于培养学生的外币真伪鉴别能力,以此保障邮轮收银工作的准确性与安全性。通过本次实训,学生将深入洞悉不同国家货币的构造特性,熟练掌握鉴别假币的有效手段,切实提升应对假币的实际操作技能,并且在服务过程中充分展现出高度的职业道德素养与宾客服务意识。

Through this task, the focus is on cultivating students' ability to identify the authenticity of foreign currencies, thereby ensuring the accuracy and security of cruise ship cashier work. Through this practical training, students will gain an in-depth understanding of the structural characteristics of currencies from different countries, proficiently master effective methods for identifying counterfeit currencies, effectively enhance their practical operating skills in dealing with counterfeit money, and fully demonstrate a high level of professional ethics and customer service awareness during the service process.

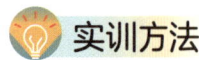
实训方法
Training Method

实训将采用理论讲解与实践操作相结合的模式。首先,教师会针对外币的特征、流通状况展开详细阐释。随后,学生通过观摩教师的示范过程,学习外币鉴别技巧。紧接着,在教师的悉心指导下,学生对外币展开实际的观察与操作,以练习鉴别技能。不仅如此,实训内容还涵盖模拟收银场景,要求学生在限定时间内完成货币真伪的鉴别任务。

The training will adopt a combination of theoretical explanation and practical operation. First of all, the teacher will elaborate in detail on the characteristics of foreign currencies and their circulation situations. Subsequently, students will learn the identification techniques by observing the teacher's demonstration. Immediately after that, under the careful guidance of the teacher, students will conduct actual observation and operation on foreign currencies to practice the identification skills. Moreover, the training content will also cover simulated cashier scenarios, requiring students to complete the identification of currency authenticity within a limited time.

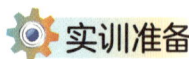
实训准备
Training Preparation

紫外灯、验钞机、美元、欧元、日元、韩元、英镑等。

Ultraviolet lamp, currency detector, US dollars, Euros, Japanese yen, South Korean won, British pounds, etc.

实训内容及操作标准
Training Content and Operating Standards

学生们将学习运用观察、触摸等方法,对货币真伪进行初步判断,包括通过视觉检查货币的颜色与图案,利用触觉感受纸张质地及凹凸印刷效果,以及通过敲击硬币来辨别其声音特征。此外,实训内容还包括专业工具的使用,如紫外灯和验钞机,借助这些工具,学生鉴别货币真伪的准确性将得到进一步提升。

Students will be taught how to use multiple senses for preliminary judgment of currency authenticity, including visual inspection of the color and patterns of the currency, feeling the paper quality and embossing through touch, and identifying sounds by tapping coins. Additionally, the training will cover the use of professional tools such as ultraviolet lamps and counterfeit detectors, which will further enhance the students' accuracy in identifying the authenticity of currency.

在掌握了基本的鉴别技巧并熟悉工具使用方法后,学生们将投身于模拟收银场景的实践中。这一环节将着重考验他们对所学知识的实际运用能力,要求他们在压力环境下做出快速且准确的判断。在模拟操作过程中,学生们还需要学会在发现假币时,采取一系列正确的应急处理措施,其中涵盖对假币的记录、及时报告以及妥善隔离等操作,以此确保交易的安全性,维护邮轮公司的良好声誉。具体程序如下:

After mastering the basic identification skills and tool usage, students will participate in simulated cashier scenarios, which will test their ability to apply the knowledge they have learned and make quick and accurate judgments under pressure. During the simulation, students will also need to learn the correct emergency handling measures to take when counterfeit currency is discovered, including recording, reporting without delay, and isolating counterfeit money to ensure the safety of transactions and the reputation of the cruise company. The specific procedures are as follows:

一、外币真假鉴别的程序
Procedure for Identification of Foreign Currency Authenticity

1. 准备(Prepare)

准备各种面额的真币样本以及紫外灯、验钞机等。

Prepare genuine currency samples of various denominations, ultraviolet lamps, currency detectors, etc.

2. 观察法(Observational Method)

直接用肉眼检查纸币的颜色、图案、肖像和文字是否清晰,颜色是否鲜艳。

Check directly with the naked eye whether the colors, patterns, portraits and texts on the banknotes are clear and whether the colors are vivid.

3. 触感法(Touch Method)

用手触摸纸币,感受纸张的厚度、质地和是否有特殊的凹凸感。

Touch the banknotes with your hands to feel the thickness and texture of the paper and whether there is a special embossed feeling.

4. 透光检查法(Transillumination Inspection Method)

将纸币对准强光源,如日光或台灯,观察水印图案是否与真币相符。

Hold the banknotes up to a strong light source, such as sunlight or a desk lamp, and observe whether the watermark pattern matches that of a genuine banknote.

5. 倾斜观察(Tilted Observation)

手持纸币,从不同角度倾斜观察,检查是否有颜色变化或隐藏图案出现。

Hold the banknote and observe it at different angles while tilting it to check whether there are color changes or hidden patterns emerging.

6. 紫外灯检测(Ultraviolet Lamp Detection)

使用紫外灯照射纸币,观察是否有防伪荧光标记或图案出现。

Shine an ultraviolet lamp on the banknote to observe whether there are anti-counterfeiting fluorescent marks or patterns appearing.

7.专业工具检测(Professional Tool Detection)

使用专业验钞机对纸币进行检测,这些机器可以检测多种安全特征。

Use professional currency detectors to test banknotes. These machines can detect a variety of security features.

8.总结(Summary)

在模拟收银环境中,练习使用上述鉴别技巧,提高实际操作能力。

Practice using the above-mentioned identification techniques in a simulated cashier environment to improve practical operation skills.

外币真假鉴别步骤图解
Step Diangram of Foreign Currency Authenticity Identification

1.准备真币样本以及紫外灯、验钞机
Prepare Samples of Genuine Currency, as Well as Ultraviolet Lamps and Currency Detectors

2.观察纸币的颜色、图案、肖像和文字是否清晰,颜色是否鲜艳
Observe Whether the Colors, Patterns, Portraits and Texts on the Banknote are Clear, and Whether the Colors Are Vivid

3.手触摸纸币,感受纸张的厚度、质地和是否有特殊的凹凸感
Touch the Banknote with Your Hand to Feel the Thickness and Texture of the Paper and Check if There Is a Special Embossed Feeling

4.将纸币对准强光源,如日光或台灯,观察水印图案是否与真币相符
Aim the Banknote at a Strong Light Source, Such as Sunlight or a Table Lamp, and Observe Whether the Watermark Pattern Matches That of a Genuine Banknote

模块7　邮轮收银服务
Module 7　Cruise Bill Settlement

5.手持纸币,从不同角度
倾斜观察,检查是否有颜色
变化或隐藏图案出现
Hold the Banknote in Hand
and Observe It from Different
Angles by Tilting It to Check if
There Is Any Color Change or
if Hidden Patterns Appear

6.使用专业验钞机对纸币进行检测,
这些机器可以检测多种
安全特征
Use Professional Currency
Detectors to Test Banknotes.
These Machines Can Detect
a Variety of Security Features

 实训任务考核指南
Training Task Assessment Guide

实训任务 Training Task	分值(分) Score (Points)	实际得分 Actual Score
仪器检查 Instrument Inspection	10	
观察法操作 Observational Method Operating	20	
触感法操作 Touch Method Operating	20	
紫外灯操作 Ultraviolet Lamp Operating	20	
专业工具操作 Professional Tool Operating	30	
【合计】 Total	100	

任务 2 外币兑换
Mission 2
Foreign Currency Exchange

实训目的
Training Objectives

本任务旨在向学生传授外币兑换的基本流程与操作技巧,确保学生在邮轮收银服务中能够精准、高效地完成外币兑换工作。

This task aims to impart to students the basic procedures and operational techniques of foreign currency exchange, ensuring that students can accurately and efficiently complete the foreign currency exchange tasks in the cashier service on cruise ships.

实训方法
Training Method

实训将采用理论讲解与实践操作相结合的方式。首先,通过教师的示范与讲解,学生将了解外币兑换的标准操作流程,包括汇率查询、服务费说明、兑换操作及后续换回操作等环节。随后,学生将通过操作电脑,开展模拟货币兑换交易实践。

The training will adopt the approach of combining theoretical explanation with practical operation. First of all, through the teacher's demonstration and explanation, students will understand the standard operating procedures of foreign currency exchange, including inquiry about exchange rates, clarification of service fees, exchange operations and subsequent redemption operations, etc. Students will operate the computer to carry out simulated currency exchange transactions.

实训准备
Training Preparation

准备不同面额和国家的货币样本、电脑汇率查询软件、验钞机等。

Prepare currency samples of different denominations and from different countries, computer exchange rate inquiry software, currency detector, etc.

实训内容及操作标准
Training Content and Operating Standards

学生将借助模拟软件或电脑程序,学习外币兑换服务的完整流程。首先,学生需清晰地向宾客询问其欲兑换的货币种类与金额,并提供当日汇率信息。在服务进程中,学生务必向宾客明确阐释任何可能产生的服务费用,并在交易开展前获取宾客的确认。紧接着,学生将练习操作电脑录入交易详情,内容涵盖外币金额、所选汇率以及据此计算得出的本币金额,同时确保所有录入数据准确无误。完成兑换后,学生将进行货币交付操作,并在适用情况下,指导宾客如何进行后续的换回操作。此外,学生还将学习如何记录交易信息,包括交易日期、时间、宾客信息以及兑换金额,以此确保交易具备透明性与可追溯性,具体程序如下:

Students will learn the complete process of foreign currency exchange services through simulation software or computer programs. Initially, students are required to clearly inquire about the type and amount of currency the customer wishes to exchange, and provide current exchange rate information. During the service, students must clearly explain any potential service fees and obtain the customer's confirmation before carrying out the transaction. Then, students will practice operating the computer to input transaction details, including the amount of foreign currency, the selected exchange rate, and the calculated local currency amount, ensuring the accuracy of all entered data. After completing the exchange, students will deliver the currency and instruct the customer on how to carry out a reverse transaction, if applicable. Additionally, students will learn how to record transaction information, including the transaction date, time, customer information, and exchange amount, to ensure the transparency and traceability of the transaction. The specific procedures are as follows:

一、外币兑换的程序
Foreign Currency Exchange Procedure

1.学生练习接待宾客,详细询问宾客所需兑换的货币种类与金额。运用电脑查询并向宾客提供当日官方汇率。

Students practice receiving guests and ask about the type and amount of currency to be exchanged. They use a computer to inquire about and provide the official exchange rate of the day.

2.学生清晰地向宾客说明可能产生的服务费用,并在开展交易前获取宾客的明确确认。

Students clearly explain the possible service fees to guests and obtain the explicit confirmation from the guests before the transaction.

3.学生在电脑系统中准确输入外币金额与选定的汇率,计算得出兑换后的本币金额,并展示给宾客。

Students input the foreign currency amount and the selected exchange rate on the computer, and calculate and display the converted local currency amount to guests.

4.学生在电脑上完成交易操作,模拟打印交易凭证,随后将实际兑换后的本币交付给宾客。

Students complete the transaction on the computer, simulate and print the transaction voucher, and actually deliver the converted local currency to the guest.

5.学生记录交易的详细信息,涵盖交易日期、时间、宾客相关信息以及兑换金额等内容。

Students record the details of the transaction, including date, time, guest information and exchange amount.

实训任务考核指南
Training Task Assessment Guide

实训任务 Training Task	分值(分) Score (Points)	实际得分 Actual Score
举止仪态 Appearance	10	
沟通 Communication	30	
换汇操作 Currency Exchange Procedure	30	
凭证打印 Invoice Print	20	
交易记录 Trade Records	10	
【合计】 Total	100	

任务 3 登记信用卡
Mission 3
Credit Card Registration

实训目的
Training Objectives

本任务旨在让相关人员掌握邮轮信用卡登记服务的标准流程,这一流程涵盖信息录入、宾客身份验证、安全审核等环节,以及宾客隐私保护和数据安全。

This task aims to teach relevant personnel to master the standard procedure of credit card registration services on cruises, including information entry, guest identity verification, security review, and protection of guest privacy and data security.

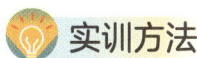

实训方法
Training Method

实训将采用理论讲解与实践操作相结合的方式。首先,通过教师的示范与讲解,学生将了解如何协助邮轮上的宾客完成信用卡登记以及与船卡的绑定等操作流程。随后,学生将运用模拟软件展开操作练习,以确保在实际工作场景中,能够熟练且准确地提供信用卡登记服务。

Practical training will employ an approach that combines theoretical explanation with practical operation. First of all, through the teacher's demonstration and explanation, students will understand how to help guests onboard the cruise ship complete the registration of credit cards and the process of binding credit cards with the ship cards. Subsequently, students will use simulation software to practice, ensuring that they can skillfully and accurately provide credit card registration services in actual work scenarios.

实训准备
Training Preparation

信用卡、船卡、宾客身份信息、模拟信用卡登记系统等。

Credit card, ship card, the guest identity information, simulation credit card registration system, etc.

实训内容及操作标准
Training Content and Operating Standards

学生将学习如何精准录入信用卡信息,实施宾客身份验证,开展信用卡安全审核,确保所有登记信息准确无误,并在邮轮系统中安全存储。此外,学生还需了解信用卡使用政策,熟练掌握异常情况处理流程,提供高标准的宾客服务,具体程序如下:

Students will learn how to precisely input credit card information, carry out guest identity verification, conduct credit card security reviews, ensure all registration information is accurate without error, and store it securely in the cruise system. In addition, students will understand credit card usage policies, master the procedures for handling exceptional situations, and provide guest services of high standard. The specific operation procedures are as follows:

一、信用卡登记的程序
Credit Card Registration Procedure

1.以专业且礼貌的态度接待每一位宾客,主动询问其是否需要使用我们的信用卡登记服务,并简要清晰地介绍该服务的相关流程与优势。

Greet every guest with professionalism and courtesy, proactively inquire whether they require our credit card registration services, and briefly and clearly introduce the relevant processes and advantages of this service.

2.仔细且精准地将宾客的信用卡信息录入我们的系统,确保信用卡卡号、有效期以及安全码(CVV)等所有关键信息完整无缺且准确无误。

Input carefully and accurately the credit card information of the guest into our system, ensuring that all key details, including the card number, expiration date, and security code (CVV), are entered without omission or error.

3.认真查验宾客提供的身份证明文件,如身份证或护照,将其与信用卡账户上的信息进行比对确保真实以及一致性。

Compare the guest's identity documents, such as an ID card or passport, with the information on the credit card account to ensure authenticity and consistency.

4.在邮轮的信用卡登记系统中,依照既定操作流程,完成宾客的信用卡登记操作。在操作的每一个步骤中,都要保持高度的精确性与细致性,确保所输入的全部数据准确无误。

Complete the guest's credit card registration in the cruise ship's credit card registration system, adhering to the established procedures. Maintain a high level of precision and attention to detail at each step to ensure that all entered data is accurate and error-free.

5.完成登记操作后,打印出信用卡登记凭证,确保凭证上的所有信息与宾客实际登记信息一致。随后,礼貌地引导宾客审阅并签字确认,以此完成整个信用卡登记流程。

After completing the registration operation, print the credit card registration voucher, ensuring that all information on the voucher matches the guest's actual registration details. Then, politely guide the guest to review and sign the voucher to finalize the credit card registration process.

信用卡登记步骤图解
Step Diagram of Credit Card Registration

1.举止仪态
Appearance

2.核对宾客身份信息
Guest Identity Information Confirm

3.信用卡信息录入
Credit Card Information Entry

4.信息确认
Information Check

实训任务考核指南
Training Task Assessment Guide

实训任务 Training Task	分值(分) Score（Points）	实际得分 Actual Score
举止仪态 Appearance	10	
核对乘客身份信息 Passenger Identity Information Confirm	10	
信用卡信息录入 Credit Card Information Entry	30	
信息确认 Information Check	30	
凭证打印 Invoice Print	20	
【合计】 Total	100	

任务 4 船上付款方式
Mission 4
Payment Method on Cruise

实训目的
Training Objectives

本任务旨在让相关人员熟悉邮轮上主要的付款方式，尤其聚焦于信用卡与储蓄卡的使用情况，同时熟练掌握这两种支付方式在操作层面的差异及对应的处理流程。

This task aims to teach relevant personnel to be familiar with the main payment methods on cruises, especially the use of credit cards and savings cards, and master the operational differences and handling processes of these two payment methods.

实训方法
Training Method

实训方法将着重于区分信用卡与储蓄卡付款方式的具体操作流程及其差异。学生首先将通过课堂讲解，了解这两种卡片的基础知识以及邮轮上的支付政策。随后，借助模拟交易练习，学生将分别针对信用卡和储蓄卡，依次练习卡片接收、刷卡操作、输入交易金额、获取宾客 PIN 码或引导宾客签名、处理授权以及完成交易等步骤。教师将引导学生识别两种卡片在实际操作中的差异，例如使用信用卡时宾客费用自动扣除，而使用储蓄卡时宾客则需在宾客服务中心进行人工扣费操作。

The training method will focus on the specific operational procedures and differences between the credit card and the savings card payment methods. Through classroom instruction, students will first understand the basic knowledge of the two cards and the payment policy on the cruise ship. Then, through simulated trading practice, students will respectively practice the steps of accepting the credit cards and the savings cards, swiping cards, inputting the transaction amount, obtaining the guest's PINs code or guiding the guest to sign, processing authorization and completing the transaction. Teachers will guide students to identify the differences between the two cards, such as the automatic deduction for guests using credit cards and the manual deduction in the guest service center for guests using savings cards.

实训准备
Training Preparation

信用卡、储蓄卡、船卡、模拟支付系统等。
Credit card, savings card, ship card, simulated payment system, etc.

实训内容及操作标准
Training Content and Operating Standards

学生将通过一系列实训流程，熟练掌握邮轮上信用卡和储蓄卡付款方式的具体操作步骤及其差异。首先，借助课堂讲解，学习这两种卡片的基础知识以及邮轮支付政策。接着，通过模拟交易练习，学生将分别针对信用卡和储蓄卡，依次练习卡片接收、刷卡操作、输入交易金额、获取宾客 PIN 码或引导宾客签名、处理授权，以及完成交易等步骤。教师将着重指导学生识别信用卡自动扣费与储蓄卡人工扣费操作的区别，并在模拟环境中练习处理交易异常情况以及提供专业的宾客服务，具体程序如下：

Students will skillfully master the specific operational processes and differences between credit and savings card payment methods on cruises through a series of practical training procedures. Students will start with classroom lectures to learn the basic knowledge of both types of cards and cruise payment policies, followed by simulated transaction exercises in which students will practice accepting cards, swiping, entering transaction amounts, obtaining guest PINs or guiding guests to sign, processing authorizations, and completing transactions. Instructors will focus on guiding students to identify the differences between automatic charging for credit cards and manual charging for savings cards, and practice handling transaction exceptions and providing professional guest service in a simulated environment.

一、船上付款的程序
Cruise Payment Procedure

1.仔细核查宾客的账单明细，保证所有费用记录准确无误。与宾客进行面对面沟通确认，确保他们对账单内容完全理解且认同。

Examine the guest's bill in detail to ensure all charges are recorded accurately. Have a face-to-face confirmation with the guest, ensuring they fully understand and agree with the bill's contents.

2.通过模拟交易场景，熟悉 POS 机的操作界面及整个交易流程。对从开始交易到完成交易的每一个步骤展开练习，确保在实际操作中能够流畅且精准地执行。

Become familiar with the POS machine's interface and the entire transaction process through simulated transaction scenarios. Practice every step from starting a transaction to completing it, ensuring smooth and accurate execution in actual operations.

3.学习信用卡后台自动结账系统的运行机制，掌握如何将信用卡交易自动结算，并及时更新宾客账户余额。确保系统能够正确处理交易,且交易结果能及时在宾客账单上体现。

Understand the operation of the credit card automatic check-out system, and master how to automatically settle credit card transactions and update the guest's account balance. Ensure the system correctly processes transactions and promptly reflects them on the guest's bill.

4.使用储蓄卡进行交易,操作包括刷卡、输入交易金额,并熟悉储蓄卡的扣费流程。向宾客清晰阐释如何进行人工扣费操作,确保他们知悉操作步骤及可能产生的费用。

Practice making transactions with savings cards, including swiping, entering transaction amounts, and getting familiar with the savings card charging process. Clearly explain to guests how to perform manual charging operations, ensuring they understand the steps and potential costs.

5.识别并处理交易过程中可能出现的异常状况,例如信用卡挂失、POS 机系统故障或宾客对账单存在争议。学习如何迅速且有效地应对这些问题,保障交易顺利推进以及宾客满意度。

Practice identifying and handling exceptional situations that may arise during transactions, such as a lost credit card, POS system malfunctions, or guest disputes over the bill. Learn how to respond effectively and quickly to these issues, ensuring smooth transactions and guest satisfaction.

船上付款步骤图解
Step Diagram of Payment Method on Cruise

1.举止仪态
Appearance

2.核对宾客账单
Guest Invoice Check

3.信用卡自动扣款操作
Automatic Payment of Credit Card

4.宾客签字确认
Guest's Signature for Confirmation

实训任务考核指南
Training Task Assessment Guide

实训任务 Training Task	分值(分) Score (Points)	实际得分 Actual Score
举止仪态 Appearance	10	
核对乘客账单 Passenger Invoice Check	10	
信用卡自动扣款操作 Automatic Payment of Credit Card	30	
储蓄卡扣款操作 Payment Operation of Savings Card	30	
异常情况处理 Abnormal Situation Handling	20	
【合计】 Total	100	

邮轮结账　项目 2

Cruise Check-out　Project 2

任务 1　邮轮结账
Mission 1　Cruise Check-out

实训目的
Training Objectives

通过教师对邮轮上结账操作程序与操作要求的讲解,学生将全面掌握邮轮结账流程中的关键环节,涵盖账单核对、支付处理以及宾客服务。学生重点学习如何在多样化的支付环境中,精准且高效地完成结账操作,以此确保宾客满意度。

Through the teacher's explanation of the check-out operation procedures and requirements on the cruise ship, students will comprehensively master the key links in the cruise check-out process, covering bill checking, payment processing, and guest services. Students will focus on learning how to accurately and efficiently complete the check-out operation in a diverse payment environment, thereby ensuring guest satisfaction.

实训方法
Training Method

本实训采用课堂讲解与实际操作相结合的方式。首先,教师将系统地讲解邮轮结账的理论知识及操作规范。接着,学生借助模拟结账系统开展实操练习,其间教师会在一旁进行指导,以确保学生能够熟练掌握结账流程中的每一个步骤。

This training will combine classroom lectures with practical operations. Initially, instructors will systematically explain the theoretical knowledge and operational standards of cruise check-out. Subsequently, students will carry out practical exercises using a simulated check-out system, during which instructors will offer guidance to ensure that students can proficiently master every step in the check-out process.

实训准备 Training Preparation

模拟账单系统、POS 机、信用卡和储蓄卡读卡器、现金模拟纸币和硬币等。

A simulated billing system, POS machines, credit and savings card readers, as well as simulated banknotes and coins, etc.

实训内容及操作标准 Training Content and Operating Standards

作为一名合格的邮轮宾客服务中心服务员,不仅要具备扎实的邮轮结账理论知识,更重要的是要掌握如何接待前来结账的宾客,仔细核对账单明细,熟练接受信用卡、储蓄卡和现金支付,并妥善处理交易。重点在于精准且迅速地完成结账操作,同时保证宾客服务的高质量。此外,还需熟练掌握多种结账方式,涵盖信用卡、储蓄卡和现金结账。针对信用卡结账,学生将学习运用相关系统进行账单核对,并执行信用卡预授权的扣除及退还操作;在储蓄卡结账环节,学生将练习引导宾客进行账单核对以及现场刷卡,认真核实交易信息,并妥善处理结账过程中可能出现的投诉或其他问题。具体程序如下:

As a qualified staff in the cruise guest service center, one should not only possess solid theoretical knowledge of cruise check-out but also, more importantly, master how to receive guests coming to check-out, check the details of the bill carefully, proficiently accept credit cards, savings cards and cash payments, and handle transactions properly. One should focus on the accuracy and speed of check-out operations and maintain high-quality guest service. Also, one needs to master a variety of check-out methods, covering credit card, savings card and cash check-out. For credit card check-out, students will learn to use relevant systems to check the bill and perform operations such as deducting and refunding the credit card pre-authorization. During the savings card check-out process, students will practice guiding guests to check the bill and swipe the card on-site, verify transaction information carefully, and properly handle complaints or other problems that may arise during check-out. The specific procedures are as follows:

一、邮轮结账的程序
Cruise Check-out Procedure

(一) 信用卡结账操作流程
Credit Card Check-out Procedure

1.账单核对:仔细核对绑定信用卡宾客的账单明细。

Bill Verification: Carefully check the detailed bill of the guest with a bound credit card.

2.在后台执行扣款操作:优先从宾客预授权金额中扣除消费款项。若预授权额度不足以支付全部消费,再从信用卡账户中扣除剩余款项。

Perform the deduction operation in the background: First, deduct the consumption amount from the guest's pre-authorization. If the pre-authorization amount is insufficient, deduct the remaining amount from the credit card account.

3.账单发送:将宾客完整的消费账单发送至其指定的邮箱地址。

Bill Delivery: Send the guest's complete consumption bill to the email address specified by the guest.

4.交易完成确认:确认交易成功后,向宾客发送交易收据。

Transaction Completion Confirmation: Upon confirming the success of the transaction, send a transaction receipt to the guest.

(二) 借记卡结账操作流程
Debit Card Check-out Procedure

1.迎接宾客:以专业且友好的态度迎接前来结账的宾客,做好结账准备工作。

Guest Greeting: Greet guests in a professional and friendly manner and make preparations for the check-out process.

2.账单核对:与宾客共同核对账单,确保所有费用明细准确无误。

Bill Verification: Check the bill with the guest to ensure that all expense details are accurate and error-free.

3.账单支付:确认宾客选择借记卡支付方式,在保障支付环境安全后,引导宾客输入密码。

Bill Settlement: Confirm that the guest chooses to pay with a debit card, and guide the guest to enter the password after ensuring the security of the payment environment.

4.确认交易:交易获批后,打印交易凭证,并请宾客签名确认。

Transaction Confirmation: After the transaction is approved, print the transaction voucher and request the guest to sign for confirmation.

5.交易完成:向宾客交付交易收据,并对宾客的支付表示感谢。

Transaction Completion: Hand over the transaction receipt to the guest and thank the guest for their payment.

实训任务考核指南
Training Task Assessment Guide

实训任务 Training Task	分值（分） Score（Points）	实际得分 Actual Score
仪容仪表、礼貌礼节 Grooming, Politeness and Etiquette	10	
账单核对 Bill Check	20	
扣款操作 Deduction Operation	20	
账单支付 Bill Payment	30	
账单发送 Bill Sending	20	
【合计】 Total	100	

案例分享
Training Content Case Studies

完美的邮轮结账体验
The Perfect Cruise Check-out Experience

在皇家加勒比"海洋量子号"的旅程接近尾声时，迎来了结账时刻。以李先生一家为例，登船时办理的房卡成为他们在船上消费的关键工具。在整个航程中，他们凭借房卡进行了各类消费，包括在餐厅用餐、购买纪念品等。

At the end of the journey on Royal Caribbean's Quantum of the Seas, the check-out time arrives. Take Mr. Li's family as an example. The room card they obtained when boarding the ship serves as a crucial tool for their onboard consumption. During the entire cruise, they utilized this room card for a wide range of expenses, such as dining at the restaurants and purchasing souvenirs.

结账前一天，李先生收到了消费明细账单，账单上详细罗列了各项消费。他在仔细核对时，发现一笔餐厅消费金额存在出入，便立即拨打客服电话说明情况。客服人员十分耐心地进行查询，最终确定是由输入失误导致，随后及时更正了错误金额。

One day before check-out, Mr. Li received a detailed consumption bill, which listed all the expenses in detail. When carefully checking the bill, he noticed a discrepancy in one of the restaurant charges. Immediately, he dialed the guest service hotline to report the situation. The customer service staff conducted a patient investigation and finally determined that it was caused by an input error. Subsequently, they promptly corrected the incorrect amount.

结账当天,李先生一家来到宾客服务中心。工作人员热情地接待了他们,并再次与李先生一同确认账单明细。李先生对更正后的账单没有异议,选择使用信用卡支付。工作人员熟练地操作POS机,完成支付流程后,为李先生打印出结账收据,收据上清晰地显示了消费总额、支付方式等信息。同时,工作人员还贴心地提醒李先生检查房卡内是否还有未结清费用,并告知房卡的归还地点。

On the day of check-out, Mr. Li's family came to the Guest Service Center. The staff greeted them warmly and once again verified the bill details with Mr. Li. Mr. Li had no objections to the corrected bill and opted to pay by credit card. The staff skillfully operated the POS machine. After completing the payment process, they printed out a check-out receipt for Mr. Li. The receipt clearly showed information such as the total consumption amount and the payment method. Meanwhile, the staff thoughtfully reminded Mr. Li to check whether there were any outstanding fees on the room card and informed him of the location for returning the room card.

李先生一家对此次结账体验感到十分满意,他们认为结账流程清晰明了,工作人员专业且高效,能够及时处理出现的问题,为他们的邮轮之旅画上了一个圆满的句号。

Mr. Li's family was extremely satisfied with this check-out experience. They believed that the check-out process was clear and straightforward, and the staff were professional and efficient. The ability to handle problems promptly brought their cruise trip to a perfect close.

模块 8

邮轮升舱换舱

Module 8

Cruise Ship Upgrade and Cabin Exchange

项目 1 邮轮升舱换舱服务
Project 1 Cruise Ship Upgrade and Cabin Exchange Service

任务 1 邮轮升舱服务
Mission 1 Cruise Cabin Upgrade Service

实训目的 Training Objectives

通过教师对邮轮上结账操作程序及操作要求的详细讲解,学生将深入领会邮轮前台升舱服务的重要意义,熟练掌握打造卓越宾客体验的关键技能。在实训过程中,学生将学习如何精准识别并充分满足宾客的需求,实现高效且有效的沟通,妥善处理宾客咨询。同时,学生还将掌握在严格遵守邮轮公司政策的前提下,如何为宾客提供免费升舱、付费升舱以及相关配套服务。

Through the teacher's detailed explanation of the operating procedures and requirements of cruise ship check-out, students will deeply comprehend the significance of the cabin upgrade service at the cruise front desk and master the key skills of providing an excellent guest experience. Through practical training, students will learn how to precisely identify and fully meet guests' needs, achieve efficient and effective communication, handle guests' inquiries, and how to provide free and paid upgrades and related services under the premise of strictly observing the policies of the cruise company.

实训方法
Training Method

本实训将采用课堂讲解与实际操作相结合的方式。首先,教师将系统地介绍邮轮结账的理论知识和操作规范。随后,学生将通过模拟邮轮客舱预订系统进行实操练习,教师将在旁指导,确保学生能够熟练掌握邮轮升舱服务中的每一个步骤。

This training will adopt a combination of classroom instruction and hands-on practice. First, the instructor will systematically introduce the theoretical knowledge and operational norms of cruise ship check-out. Subsequently, students will conduct practical exercises through a simulated cruise cabin reservation system, with the instructor providing on-site guidance to ensure that students can proficiently master every step in the cruise upgrade service.

实训准备
Training Preparation

模拟前台接待区、预订系统、POS 机、客舱分配表、升舱政策手册等。

Prepare simulated versions of the front desk reception area, reservation system, POS machine, cabin allocation table, and cabin upgrade policy manual, etc.

实训内容及操作标准
Training Content and Operating Standards

作为一名合格的邮轮宾客服务中心服务员,不仅要具备扎实的邮轮客舱理论知识,更重要的是要熟练掌握宾客付费升舱和免费升舱的相关操作流程。在处理付费升舱请求时,首先需确认宾客当前所入住的客舱类型以及他们期望升级到的目标客舱类型。借助预订系统查询目标客舱的可预订状态,并依据邮轮公司的升舱政策准确计算所需支付的额外费用。向宾客详细阐释升舱所能带来的诸多益处,例如更豪华的设施配备、更优质的服务体验等。一旦宾客同意升舱,熟练操作 POS 机完成支付流程,并及时在系统中更新宾客的客舱信息。确保宾客顺利领取新的房卡以及详细的升舱收据,同时清晰告知他们前往新客舱的路线指引。在整个服务过程中,始终保持专业的服务态度和礼貌的沟通方式,切实让宾客感受到个性化、定制化的服务。

As a qualified staff member in the cruise guest service center, one should not only possess solid theoretical knowledge of cruise cabins but also, more importantly, be proficient in the relevant operating procedures for both paid and free cabin upgrades. When handling a paid upgrade request, the first step is to confirm the current cabin type of the guest and the target cabin type to which they wish to upgrade. Utilize the reservation system to check the availability of the target cabin and accurately calculate the additional charges in accordance with the cruise company's upgrade policy. Elaborate in detail to the guest on the numerous benefits of upgrading, such as more luxurious facilities and a higher-quality service experience. Once the guest consents to the upgrade, skillfully operate the POS machine to complete the payment process and promptly update the guest's cabin information in the system. Ensure that the guest smoothly obtains the new room card and a detailed upgrade receipt, and clearly inform them of the directions to the new cabin. Throughout the entire service process, maintain a professional service attitude and polite communication style at all times, so as to truly make the guest feel a personalized and customized service.

若宾客希望使用其权益或积分进行免费升舱,服务员需仔细核实宾客的会员资格以及积分余额。清晰展示可供宾客用积分兑换的客舱类型,并详细解释积分兑换的政策和具体操作程序。在宾客选定升舱方案后,通过预订系统精准完成积分兑换操作,同时及时更新宾客的客舱信息。为宾客发放新的客舱卡,并确认他们清楚了解新客舱的设施配备以及所包含的各项服务。在整个服务过程中,着重强调宾客享有的会员权益,切实确保他们能充分感受到作为忠诚宾客所拥有的尊贵体验。具体程序如下:

If guests wish to use their entitlements or points for a free cabin upgrade, the service staff need to carefully verify the guests' membership status and point balances. Clearly display the cabin types available for point redemption and explain in detail the point-redemption policies and specific operating procedures. After the guest selects an upgrade option, accurately complete the point-redemption operation through the reservation system and promptly update the guest's cabin information. Issue new cabin cards to the guests and confirm that they clearly understand the facilities in the new cabin and all the services included. Throughout the entire service process, place emphasis on the membership entitlements of the guests to effectively ensure that they fully experience the privileged treatment as loyal guests. The specific procedures are as follows:

一、邮轮升舱的程序
Procedures for Upgrading A Cruise Ship Cabin

(一) 付费升舱操作流程
Operating Process of Paid Cabin Upgrade

1.确认宾客需求:详细询问宾客当前所居住的客舱类型,以及他们期望升级至的目标客舱类型。

Confirm the guest's needs: ask the guest about the current cabin type and the target cabin type they wish to upgrade to.

2.查询客舱可用性:通过预订系统仔细检查目标客舱是否处于可预订状态。

Inquire about cabin availability: carefully check the availability of the target cabin in the reservation system.

3.计算额外费用:严格依据邮轮公司既定政策,精确计算出升舱所需支付的额外费用。

Calculate the extra cost: calculate the additional cost for the cabin upgrade in strict accordance with the established policy of the cruise company.

4.升舱设施介绍:向宾客清晰且全面地介绍升舱后能够享受到得更为豪华的设施以及

更为优质的服务。

Introduction of Upgrade Facilities：clearly and comprehensively introduce the more luxurious facilities and better services that guests can enjoy after upgrading.

5.处理支付：在宾客明确同意升舱后，熟练运用POS机妥善处理支付相关事宜。

Handle Payment：after the guest clearly agrees to the upgrade, skillfully use a POS machine to properly handle payment-related matters.

6.提供新的房卡：立即向宾客发放新的房卡，以此作为升舱已完成的确认凭证。

Provide a New Room Card：promptly provide guests with a new room card as confirmation of the completed upgrade.

7.指引新客舱位置：清晰告知宾客前往他们新客舱的具体路线和方式。

Guide to the New Cabin Location：clearly inform guests of the specific route and method to get to their new cabin.

（二）使用权益或积分进行免费升舱操作流程
Free Cabin Upgrade Operation Process Using Rights or Points

1.确认宾客需求：详细询问宾客当前所居住的客舱类型，以及他们期望升级到的目标客舱类型。

Confirm the Guest's Needs：ask the guest about the current cabin type and the target cabin type they wish to upgrade to.

2.核实会员资格和积分：仔细确认宾客的会员身份，以及其账户内可用的积分余额。

Verify Membership and Points：carefully confirm the guest's membership status and the available points balance in the guest's account.

3.展示可兑换客舱：清晰地向宾客展示，基于他们现有的积分能够兑换的客舱类型。

Show Redeemable Cabins：clearly show guests the types of cabins for which their points can be redeemed.

4.解释兑换政策：全面且清晰地向宾客介绍积分兑换的政策内容，以及具体的操作程序。

Explain the Redemption Policy：comprehensively and clearly introduce the points redemption policy and procedures to guests.

5.完成积分兑换：当宾客确定选择升舱方案后，在预订系统中精准无误地完成积分兑换操作。

Complete Point Redemption：after the guest chooses to upgrade, accurately complete the point redemption operation in the reservation system.

6.更新并确认客舱信息：及时更新宾客的新客舱信息，同时向宾客确认，确保他们清楚了解新客舱所配备的设施以及提供的服务。

Update and Confirm Cabin Information：promptly update guests' new cabin information and confirm that they understand the facilities and services in the new cabin.

7.提供新的房卡：为宾客发放新的房卡，以此作为升舱成功的确认凭证。

Provide a New Room Card：provide guests with a new room card as confirmation of a successful upgrade.

8.指引新客舱位置：明确告知宾客前往新客舱的具体路线及方式。

Guide to the New Cabin Location: clearly tell guests the specific route and method to get to their new cabin.

邮轮升舱步骤图解

Step Diagram of Upgrading a Cruise Ship Cabin

1.升舱政策说明与条件评估
Cabin Upgrade Policy Explanation and Eligibility

2.可用升舱选项展示
Available Cabin Upgrade Options

3.升舱费用计算及手续办理
Cabin Upgrade Fee Calculation and Cabin Upgrade Operating

4.支付操作
Payment Operation

5.更新房卡
Renew Room Card

实训任务考核指南
Training Task Assessment Guide

实训任务 Training Task	分值(分) Score（Points）	实际得分 Actual Score
仪容仪表、礼貌礼节 Grooming, Politeness and Etiquette	10	
升舱政策说明与条件评估 Upgrade Policy Explanation and Eligibility	20	
可用升舱选项展示 Available Upgrade Options	20	
升舱费用计算 Upgrade Fee Calculation	10	
升舱手续办理 Upgrade Operating	10	
支付操作 Payment Operation	10	
更新房卡 Renew Room Card	10	
操作时间 Operating Time	10	
【合计】 Total	100	

任务 2　邮轮换舱服务
Mission 2
Cruise Cabin Exchange Service

实训目的
Training Objectives

学生将系统且全面地掌握邮轮换舱服务的完整操作流程，显著提升宾客服务技能，深入学习如何在严格遵循邮轮公司政策的基础上，为宾客提供高效且专业的换舱服务。

Students will systematically and thoroughly master the complete operation process of cruise cabin exchange services, significantly enhance their guest-service skills, and learn how to provide efficient and professional cabin exchange services while strictly adhering to the policies of the cruise company.

实训方法
Training Method

实训将综合运用课堂讲解、角色扮演、模拟操作以及案例分析等多种教学方法，切实保障学生能够透彻理解并熟练掌握换舱服务的每一个环节。

The training will comprehensively employ a variety of teaching methods such as classroom instruction, role-playing, simulation-based operations, and case studies to effectively ensure that students can thoroughly comprehend and proficiently master each aspect of the cabin exchange service.

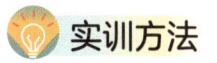

实训准备
Training Preparation

模拟前台接待区、预订系统、POS 机、客舱分配表、换舱政策手册等。

Prepare simulated versions of the front desk reception area, reservation system, POS machine, cabin allocation chart, and cabin exchange policy manual.

实训内容及操作标准
Training Content and Operating Standards

在邮轮换舱服务实训中,学生将深入学习如何以专业且周到的方式,妥善处理宾客基于客观或主观原因所提出的换舱请求。首先,学生务必掌握耐心倾听宾客具体诉求的技巧,无论这些诉求源自客舱设施故障、周遭环境干扰,抑或是个人特殊偏好等因素,都要一丝不苟地认真记录,并充分展现出感同身受的同理心。紧接着,学生需依据邮轮公司既定的换舱政策,向宾客清晰、详尽地阐释可能存在的条件限制、相关费用明细以及切实可行的解决方案。在确认可行的换舱方案后,学生将着手练习在预订系统中精准查询客舱的可用状态,积极协调相关部门完成新客舱的筹备工作,并为宾客高效办理换舱手续。除此之外,学生还将学习如何全方位协助宾客完成搬迁过程,切实保障其行李及个人物品安全转移至新客舱,并且在搬迁完成后,及时给予必要的关怀与支持,包括主动跟进宾客的满意度情况,以及在必要时提供额外服务或合理补偿。在整个服务流程中,学生将持续练习保持专业、高效的服务标准,确保每一位宾客都能深切感受到被重视、被尊重。具体程序如下:

In the cruise cabin exchange service training, students will deeply learn how to handle guests' cabin exchange requests resulting from objective or subjective reasons in a professional and considerate manner. First, students must master the skill of listening patiently to guests' specific demands. Whether these demands stem from cabin facility malfunctions, environmental interferences, or personal special preferences, students should record them meticulously and fully demonstrate empathetic understanding. Subsequently, based on the established cabin exchange policy of the cruise company, students need to clearly and comprehensively explain to guests the possible conditional restrictions, detailed relevant fees, and practical solutions. After confirming a feasible cabin exchange plan, students will start to practice accurately checking the availability status of cabins in the reservation system, actively coordinate with relevant departments to complete the preparation work for the new cabin, and efficiently handle the cabin exchange formalities for guests. Moreover, students will also learn how to comprehensively assist guests in the moving process, effectively ensure the safe transfer of their luggage and personal items to the new cabin, and promptly provide necessary care and support after the move, including actively following up on guests' satisfaction and providing additional services or reasonable compensation when necessary. Throughout the entire service process, students will continuously practice maintaining professional and efficient service standards, ensuring that every guest can deeply feel valued and respected. The specific procedures are as follows:

一、邮轮换舱的程序
Procedure of Cruise Cabin Exchange

1.询问与评估:首先,需耐心询问宾客希望换舱的具体缘由,例如客舱设施出现故障、

存在噪声干扰等情况。全面评估宾客的换舱请求是否合理,同时仔细检查是否存在客观证据,用以支撑宾客所陈述的情况。

Inquiry and Assessment:begin by patiently inquiring of the guests about the specific reasons they wish to change cabins, such as malfunctions of cabin facilities or noise disturbances. Assess whether the guests' requests are reasonable and check for objective evidence supporting their statements.

2.查询与协调:在确认宾客请求具有合理性之后,即刻查询其他客舱的可使用状态。积极与相关部门展开协调工作,全力确保能够切实满足宾客的换舱需求。

Check and Coordinate:after confirming the validity of the guests' requests, immediately check the availability of other cabins. Actively coordinate with relevant departments to fully ensure that the cabin exchange demand of the guests can be effectively met.

3.办理换舱:若换舱方案切实可行,应迅速且高效地为宾客办理换舱手续。及时在系统中更新宾客的新客舱信息,并同步通知相关部门,诸如客房服务部门等。

Process the Change:if feasible, promptly and efficiently process the cabin change for the guests. Update the guests' new cabin information in the system and simultaneously notify relevant departments such as housekeeping.

4.协助搬迁:妥善安排工作人员协助宾客搬迁至新客舱,务必确保宾客的行李以及个人物品安全、完整地转移至新舱位。

Assist in Relocation:appropriately arrange for staff to assist guests in relocating to the new cabin and ensure that the luggage and personal items of the guests are transferred to the new cabin safely and intactly.

5.后续关怀:在宾客完成搬迁之后,主动跟进宾客的满意度情况,并依据实际情形提供必要的额外服务或合理补偿,以此充分确保宾客能够拥有舒适体验并感到满意。

Follow-up Care:after the guests have moved, actively follow up on their satisfaction situation and provide necessary additional services or reasonable compensation according to the actual situation to ensure their comfort and satisfaction.

邮轮换舱步骤图解
Step Diagram of Cruise Cabin Change

1.询问与评估
Inquiry and Assessment

2.查询与协调
Check and Coordinate

3.办理换舱
Process the Change

4.支付操作　　　　　　　　　　　　5.更新房卡
Payment Operation　　　　　　　　Renew Room Card

实训任务考核指南
Training Task Assessment Guide

实训任务 Training Task	分值（分） Score（Points）	实际得分 Actual Score
仪容仪表、礼貌礼节 Grooming, Politeness and Etiquette	10	
接待与需求确认 Reception and Needs Confirmation	20	
客舱系统模拟查询 Cabin System Simulation Query	20	
办理换舱手续 Handling of Cabin Change Procedures	30	
更新房卡 Renew Room Card	10	
操作时间 Operating Time	10	
【合计】 Total	100	

案例分享
Training Content Case Studies

一、皇家加勒比"海洋量子号""皇家套房"特色揭秘
The "Royal Suite" on Royal Caribbean's Quantum of the Seas is a Model of Luxury at Sea

踏入套房,映入眼帘的便是开阔敞亮的客厅,高档考究的装修风格,搭配上触感柔软的地毯,相得益彰。大型沙发组合与精致小巧的茶几,彼此呼应,和谐融洽。超大尺寸的高清电视以及先进前沿的音响系统,为宾客带来极致的视听盛宴。独立设置的用餐区,摆放着一张豪华大气的餐桌,能够轻松容纳多人同时就餐。在璀璨华丽的吊灯映照下,营造出优雅迷人的用餐氛围,令人陶醉其中。

Upon entering the suite, one is immediately struck by the spacious and bright living room. The high-end decoration, combined with the soft carpet, makes the large sofa set and the exquisite coffee table complement each other perfectly. The oversized high-definition TV and advanced audio system bring the ultimate audio-visual enjoyment. The independent dining area has a luxurious dining table that can accommodate multiple people, which creates an elegant and enchanting dining atmosphere under the glow of the magnificent chandelier.

卧室之中,配备了一张超大号的舒适双人床,顶级品质的床垫,搭配高支数的纯棉床上用品,确保宾客每一晚都能拥有优质惬意的睡眠体验。床头背景墙设计独具匠心,以其独特的风格,巧妙地增添了浓郁的艺术气息。独立衣帽间不仅空间宽敞,而且设计布局极为合理。卫生间采用了干湿分离的贴心设计,淋浴区配备了高档喷头与按摩花洒,浴缸区设有超大尺寸的按摩浴缸,双洗手盆的配置尽显奢华与便利。整个卫生间采用高档石材进行装饰,质感十足,彰显尊贵品位。

The bedroom is equipped with an oversized and comfortable double bed. The top-quality mattress paired with high-count cotton bedding ensures guests enjoy a high-quality and cozy sleep experience every night. The uniquely designed bedside background wall adds a rich artistic flavor, and the independent cloakroom is spacious and reasonably designed. The bathroom has a dry-wet separation design. The high-end showerhead and massage shower in the shower area, the oversized massage bathtub in the bathtub area, and the double washbasins all show luxury and comfort. The use of high-grade stone materials for decoration further showcases the luxurious texture.

入住"皇家套房"的宾客,可享有优先登船与离船的专属特权,更有专属管家全程提供贴心周到的服务,涵盖从预订餐厅、安排船上活动等各个生活细节。房内的免费迷你吧,精心准备了丰富多样的饮品与美味小吃,每日还会定时送上新鲜的水果与娇艳的鲜花。套房内配备免费的高速无线网络。此外,还设有专属贵宾休息室,为宾客提供舒适惬意的座椅,以及丰富多彩的专属娱乐活动。在餐饮方面,宾客可尽情享受专属餐厅提供的用餐服务,全方位、多层次地为宾客带来尊贵非凡的体验,让这段海上之旅成为宾客心中

一段无比难忘的美好回忆。

  Guests staying in the "Royal Suite" can enjoy the privileges of priority boarding and disembarkation. There is an exclusive butler who provides considerate services throughout the whole process, covering details such as booking restaurants and arranging on-board activities. The room is equipped with a free mini-bar that offers a variety of drinks and delicious snacks. Fresh fruits and delicate flowers are also delivered daily. The suite is equipped with free high-speed Wi-Fi. There is also an exclusive VIP lounge that provides comfortable seats and exclusive entertainment activities. In terms of catering, guests can enjoy the exclusive restaurant dining service, bringing guests a comprehensive and extraordinary noble experience, making this sea journey an extremely unforgettable memory in their hearts.

附录 邮轮前厅英语词汇
Appendix English Vocabulary of Cruise Front Office

A

Aft/forward：往船尾叫"aft"，往船头叫"forward"
Available berth：可售舱房
Abandon ship alarm：弃船信号
Abandon ship drill：弃船演习
Adaptor：转换接头
Adventure cruise：探险航次
Atrium：中庭（邮轮中间楼层的主要公共空间）
Auditory assistance：听力帮助
Assisted listening devices：助听设备
Assembly station：集合点
Accessible gaming（casino）：无障碍赌场
Accessible showroom seating：演出室无障碍座位
Accessible public areas：无障碍的公共区域
Accessible public restrooms：无障碍的公共厕所
Assistant guest service manager/assistant guest manager：邮轮前厅部副经理

B

Beverage：饮料
Bow/stern：船的前半部分叫"bow"，船的后半部分叫"stern"
Booking form：预订表格
Booking on board：船上预订
Bunker adjustment factor（BAF）：燃油附加费
Baggage policy：行李条款
Bellboy：行李员
Board：登船
Boarding pass：登船卡、登船通行证

Bibby cabin:特等舱房
Boutique ship:精品邮轮,全部都是套房
Braille signage:盲文标牌
Buffet restaurant:自助餐厅
Butler:私人管家

C

Cabin:客舱
Cabin steward:客舱服务员
Closed-loop sailing:指出发和返回都是同一个港口的邮轮航程
Cabin balcony:客舱阳台
Cabin voltage:舱内电压
Captain's cocktail party:船长鸡尾酒会
Captain's farewell dinner:船长告别晚宴
Captain's welcome dinner:船长欢迎晚宴
Cashless:非现金的、无现金的
Casual dress:非正式着装
Check-in:入住
Check-out:退房
Clearance officer:签证官
Ceiling pullman:上铺,通常可折叠于舱壁
Convertable lower beds:下铺可合并为大床的两个单人床
Comments card:意见卡
Commission policy:佣金条款
Complaint:投诉
Concierge:礼宾服务,宾客礼宾关系
Concierge lounge/club:礼宾俱乐部
Credit card:信用卡
Credit watch:信用警告
Crew laundry:邮轮上负责洗衣的服务员
Crew mess:船员餐厅
Crew quarter:船员宿舍,宾客不能擅入
Crew only:船员专区,宾客不能擅入
Cruise guide:航程指南
Cruise director:负责船上娱乐工作的服务人员
Cruise tour:由邮轮公司提供的巴士岸上观光行程
Captain:船长,船上的最高指挥官
Cruise documents:邮轮船票、行李牌等相关资料文件

Cruise counselor：邮轮顾问

Cruise staff：邮轮员工

Cruise schedule：航班

Cruise terminal：邮轮码头

Cruise tour：邮轮旅游

Cruise tickets/E-ticket：邮轮船票、电子船票

Category：类别、种类，如内舱房、海景房等

Capacity utilization：入住率，舱位利用率

Charter：包船

Charter party：包船契约

Charter purchase：包船租购协议

Consultation：咨询

D

Daily program：船上日程表

Deck：甲板

Deck plan：甲板布置图（每一层的空间平面图）

Disembarkation：离船、下船

Downgrade：降低舱位

Debarkation：下船

Dealer：荷官

Documentation officer/administration officer：证件管理专员

Dress code：着装代码

Duty-free shops：免税店

Dry cleaning/laundry service：干洗/洗衣服务

E

Embarkation：登船、上船

Embarkation counter/check-in counter：登记柜台

Embarkation day：登船日

Embarkation department：登船部

Embarkation lunch：登船午餐

Embarkation ladder：登船梯

Embarkation agent：登船代理

Embarkation officer：登船专员

Early bird booking：早鸟预订
Emergency broadcasting：紧急广播
Emergency card：应急卡
Entertainment：休闲娱乐
Evacuation order：逃生顺序

F

Friends of bill W：船上匿名酒会的代名词
Fly cruise：长线邮轮旅游
Full-ship charter：整包船
Family cabin：家庭套房
Fitness center/GYM：健身中心/健身
Fire escape：防火逃生梯
First seating：第一批次用餐
Formal dress：正式着装
Formal night：正装之夜
Future cruise sales/next cruise：未来航程销售，下次航程销售
Front desk manager/guest relations manager：前台部经理

G

Galley：邮轮厨房
Gangway：邮轮码头和邮轮之间让游客上下船用的那段舷梯
Group coordinator：团队协调员
Guarantee：担保预订
Guest services 宾客服务
Guest service department：宾客服务部，即邮轮前厅部
Guest relations desk：宾客服务台，即邮轮前台
Guest service desk：宾客服务台，即邮轮前台
Guest service manager/front office manager：邮轮前厅部经理

H

Helideck：直升机甲板

Hotel manager:酒店部经理
Home port:母港

I

In-cabin calling:舱内直拨电话
In-cabin magazine:舱内杂志
Inside cabin:内舱房
Internet center:网吧
International host or hostess/ambassador:国际翻译专员
Inaugural cruise:新船首航
Itinerary:行程

L

Lido deck:丽都甲板,即游泳池甲板
Liner keeper:舱房床品保管员
Life boat:救生艇
Life raft:救生筏
Lifebuoy:救生圈
Life jacket:救生衣
Life preserver:救生用具
Life saving equipment:救生设备
Lobby deck:大堂甲板
Logo shop:纪念品店
Lower berth:下铺
Library:图书馆
Loyalty program:忠诚顾客计划
Luggage tag:行李牌

M

Maiden voyage:处女航,首航
MDR:main dining room 的缩写,是指邮轮上的主餐厅
Muster drill/muster station:紧急集合演习或紧急集合地点
Manifest:船上船员及游客名单

O

Ocean view stateroom:海景房
Ocean view stateroom with balcony:阳台房
Onboard:登船、上船
Onboard credit(OBC):船上消费额
Onboard currency:船上通用货币
Onboard/shipboard account:船上消费账户
Onboard revenue:船上消费收入
One piece evening gown:女士连身一体式晚礼服
Online check-in/Web check-in:网上登记
Operator:接线员、话务员
Open-jaw sailing:单向巡航,出发和返回不在同一个港口
Open seating:开放式用餐
Outside cabin:外舱房
Owner's suite:专属套房,或主人套房

P

Port/starboard:航海术语一般把左边称为"port",右边称为"starboard"
Porthole:舷窗
Purser:收银员,主管财务和结算
Passenger boarding bridge:游客登船桥
Pre and post cruise package:巡航前后的套餐
Port agent:港口代理
Port authority:港务局
Port briefing/talk:港口说明会
Port day:靠港日
Port of call:挂靠港、访问港或停靠港
Port of departure:始发港
Port of destination:目的地港
Port of entry:入境港
Port of registry:船籍港
Pre-sold shore:预售的岸上观光行程
Pax:乘客 passenger 的缩写
Passengers space ratio:游客空间比率
Passenger profile:游客资料概况

Priority check-in：优先登船
Promenade：长廊,步行街,步行道
Promenade deck：服务设施甲板

Q

Quad share：四人间

R

Restaurant：餐厅
Receptionist：邮轮前台接待员
Repositioning or repo cruise：转港航线
Ratio of staff to passengers：船员与游客的比例
Room service：客舱服务,特指客舱送餐
Room attendant：客舱服务员
Room move：舱房更换

S

Safe：保险箱
Sea bands：防晕带
Sea day：海上航行日
Sea pass card：邮轮登船卡、邮轮船卡、邮轮房卡
Second seating：第二批次用餐
Secondary consumption：二次消费
Self-service laundry：自助洗衣服务
Shipboard announcements：船上广播
Shore excursion：岸上观光
Shore excursion desk/tour desk：岸上观光预订台
Shoulder season：邮轮平季
Sign on：签到,船员登船
Sign off：签退,船员离船
Specialty restaurant：付费餐厅
Stateroom：客舱,特指游客的舱房
Staterooms with wide doors：适合轮椅进出的宽门客舱
Staterooms with low or no doorsills：低门槛或者无门槛的客舱

Suite：套房
Sun/sports deck：运动甲板

T

Table card：餐席卡
Tender boat：接驳船、摆渡船
Transit passengers：中转游客
Traditional dining：传统用餐
Turnaround day：离船/登船日

U

Upgrade：舱位升级、舱房升级

V

VIP service：贵宾接待服务
Voyage charter：航次包船
Veranda cabin：阳台舱
Visual assistance（visually impaired）：视力帮助

W

Water sports：水上运动
World cruise：环球航线
Wrap-around promenade：运动甲板上的环形跑步道
Wheelchair passengers accepted：轮椅游客可选
Wheelchair passengers must be accompanied：轮椅游客必选

参考文献
References

[1] 李肖楠,徐文苑.邮轮前厅服务与管理[M].北京:化学工业出版社,2020.

[2] 柴勤芳,姚丹丽.邮轮休闲娱乐服务管理[M].3版.大连:大连海事大学出版社,2022.

[3] 孙玉琴,甘胜军.邮轮运营管理[M].北京:旅游教育出版社,2020.

[4] 林增学,胡顺利.邮轮客舱服务管理[M].大连:大连海事大学出版社,2023.